Dissuading war mongers

DM Ole Kiminta

Published by DM Ole Kiminta, 2024.

While every precaution has been taken in the preparation of this book, the publisher assumes no responsibility for errors or omissions, or for damages resulting from the use of the information contained herein.

DISSUADING WAR MONGERS

First edition. November 5, 2024.

ISBN: 979-8227324368

Written by DM Ole Kiminta.

Also by DM Ole Kiminta

How the Western Democracies failed the world
How the Western Democracies failed the world
Shadows in the water: Supporting refugees in their homelands
Availing Concerted global responsibility for Afghan women's rights
Tethered to the kitchen: Concerted global responsibility for Afghanistan women's rights
Dissuading Global War Mongers:
Dissuading war mongers

Table of Contents

For:

Vickie Kiminta

Irene Kiminta

Catherine Kiminta

Rawan Nasreddine

Chapter 1

There are many ways of morphing up a case for peaceful co-existence just as there are numerous groups or countries that feel or think that there are no levels of playing field when it comes to muddying world peace. We have witnessed this repeatedly where aggressive countries or regimes choose to break every rule and ignore the global agreements that rules must be adhered to in order to protect human rights and anything else that goes against moral code of ethics. The fact that some countries are able to go after their neighbours and cause enormous harm and destruction beyond reasons just because the big brother protector will come by if the victim reacts or fights back is not an acceptable explanation to the global civil society. Silence is not GOLDEN when it comes to the suffering of human beings. Perhaps in the years to come, if we do not blow ourselves out of the galaxy, we will come to understand how wrong it was to be fired from your job just because you uttered the right words by siding with one of the warring parties. The subject of my book is the war mongers of today and yesterday and about how unthoughtful we have become after two world wars which should never have happened. It is not something to be proud of, but it is paradoxically human behaviour which should not be an excuse. The second half of this book is about the kind of warfare that is currently protruding from the horizon and it is not fictional, it is not an exaggeration, no, it is very current in its environmental infancy.

Understanding global warmongers necessitates an examination of the motivations and mechanisms that drive individuals and nations toward conflict. War mongers often exploit political, economic, and social grievances to justify military actions, framing them as necessary for national security or economic gain. This rhetoric can resonate deeply with the public, leading to a cycle of militarism that undermines efforts toward global peace. By dissecting the narratives employed by these entities, it becomes clear that dissuading warmongers requires not only addressing their justifications but also promoting alternative narratives that prioritise dialogue and cooperation.

The psychological impact of war extends far beyond the battlefield, affecting both combatants and civilians. War creates a pervasive climate of fear and distrust, which can manifest in long-term trauma and societal division. This psychological toll impedes global peace efforts, as communities recovering from conflict often struggle to rebuild relationships and trust. Understanding this impact is crucial for advocates of peace, as it emphasises the need for comprehensive mental health support and conflict resolution programs in post-war societies. By addressing the psychological ramifications of war, we can better facilitate healing and foster environments conducive to peace.

Economically, militarism poses significant challenges to global stability. Resources diverted to military expenditure limit investments in education, healthcare, and infrastructure, perpetuating cycles of poverty and inequality. Nations embroiled in conflict often experience economic decline, exacerbating humanitarian crises and displacement. Advocating for dissuasion of warmongers involves highlighting the long-term benefits of peace, which can lead to economic growth and stability. By promoting a shift from military spending to social investments, we can create a compelling argument for a more peaceful global framework that prioritises human development.

Historical case studies of successful peace movements provide valuable insights into effective strategies for dissuading warmongers. Movements that have emphasised nonviolent resistance, grassroots organising, and coalition-building demonstrate the power of collective action in challenging militaristic agendas. Analysing these cases reveals common themes, such as the importance of inclusivity and diverse participation, which can inspire current and future peace initiatives. Learning from the successes of past movements can empower individuals and communities to engage in constructive dialogue and activism aimed at dismantling the narratives that support war.

Environmental degradation linked to armed conflicts presents another critical angle in understanding global warmongers. Wars often lead to the destruction of ecosystems, loss of biodiversity, and pollution, further complicating already tenuous global environmental issues. The connection between militarism and environmental harm underscores the importance of integrating ecological considerations into peace efforts. Advocating for the protection of natural resources and sustainable practices can serve as a unifying point for diverse groups, emphasising that true security is intrinsically tied to environmental health. By highlighting these connections, we can cultivate a broader understanding of the stakes involved in dissuading warmongers and fostering a lasting peace which at the present time seems unreachable.

The value of world peace

THE CONCEPT OF WORLD peace holds immense value in fostering a harmonious global society. It serves as a foundation for cooperation among nations, promoting diplomacy over conflict. The importance of dissuading global war mongers is underscored by the understanding that peace allows for the resolution of disputes through dialogue and negotiation rather than violence. In an increasingly interconnected world, the consequences of warfare extend beyond borders, affecting international relations and undermining efforts to achieve lasting stability. Therefore, advocating for world peace is not merely an idealistic pursuit but a pragmatic approach to ensuring global security and cooperation.

The psychological impact of war is profound and far-reaching, influencing not only those directly involved in conflict but also societies at large. Trauma, loss, and displacement resulting from armed confrontations can lead to a cycle of violence that perpetuates hostility and distrust among nations. The mental health consequences affect generations, making it crucial to emphasize the value of peace in fostering psychological resilience. By promoting peaceful resolutions, societies can cultivate environments where individuals thrive, free from the scars of war, thereby reinforcing the importance of global peace efforts.

Economically, the consequences of militarism are detrimental to global stability. The resources allocated to military expenditures could be redirected towards development, education, and healthcare, which are essential for fostering prosperity. Nations embroiled in conflict often experience economic downturns, infrastructure destruction, and reduced foreign investment. This creates a vicious cycle where poverty and instability feed into one another. By prioritising peace, countries can focus on economic collaboration and development, leading to mutually beneficial outcomes that enhance global prosperity.

Historical case studies of successful peace movements demonstrate the feasibility and effectiveness of non-violent approaches to conflict resolution. From the civil rights movement in the United States to the anti-apartheid struggle in South Africa, these movements highlight the power of collective action and resilience in achieving social change. They reveal that peace is not only a desirable goal but an achievable one through commitment to justice and dialogue. Learning from these examples can inspire contemporary efforts to dissuade warmongers and advocate for peaceful solutions in today's conflicts.

The environmental degradation linked to armed conflicts further emphasises the urgent need for world peace. Warfare devastates ecosystems, displaces populations, and exacerbates resource scarcity, leading to long-term environmental consequences. Climate change and resource depletion are among the most pressing issues faced globally, and addressing them requires international cooperation built on peaceful relations. Additionally, the influence of media plays a significant role in shaping public perception of war and peace, often framing conflicts in sensational terms that can incite fear and hostility. By promoting narratives that emphasise the value of peace and cooperation, we can shift public discourse and create a cultural environment that prioritises understanding and resolution over conflict.

Definition and overview of war mongering

WAR MONGERING AGAINST smaller nations is defined as the aggressive political and military actions taken by more powerful countries to assert dominance, often under the guise of national security or humanitarian intervention. This behavior typically manifests through threats, coercive diplomacy, or outright military action, aiming to undermine the sovereignty and autonomy of weaker states. Understanding this phenomenon requires an exploration of the historical context in which powerful nations justify their actions, often relying on a narrative that portrays their interventions as necessary for regional stability or global security.

Throughout history, numerous case studies illustrate the repeated pattern of larger powers targeting smaller nations. Instances such as the U.S. interventions in Grenada and Panama, or Russia's actions in Georgia and Ukraine, exemplify how powerful states exploit perceived vulnerabilities in smaller ones. These interventions frequently result in significant political and social upheaval, leaving lasting scars on the affected nations. The motivations behind such actions often intertwine with economic interests, strategic geopolitical positioning, and the pursuit of ideological goals, demonstrating a complex interplay between power dynamics and international relations.

The impact of foreign intervention on the sovereignty of small nations is profound and multifaceted. Interventions often lead to the erosion of local governance structures, undermining the legitimacy of existing political institutions. As foreign powers impose their will, the resulting instability can foster internal conflict and division, further weakening the state. Additionally, the psychological toll on the population can lead to a sense of helplessness and disillusionment with national identity, as citizens grapple with the reality of external control and influence over their lives.

Propaganda techniques play a crucial role in the war mongering narrative, serving to justify the actions of aggressors while demonizing the targeted nations. These techniques may include the dissemination of misleading information, framing the narrative to highlight threats posed by the smaller nation, or portraying the intervention as a noble cause. By manipulating public perception, larger powers can rally domestic support for their actions and diminish international criticism. The effectiveness of these strategies underscores the importance of media literacy and critical thinking in an age where information is weaponised.

Nationalism often emerges as a powerful force in small nations facing aggression, shaping their responses and resilience against external pressures. In many cases, a strong sense of national identity can galvanize populations to resist foreign intervention, fostering unity and collective action. Strategies employed by small nations to counter bullying may include forming alliances with other states, leveraging international law, and appealing to global public opinion. Through these efforts, smaller nations strive to assert their sovereignty and challenge the narrative imposed by more powerful adversaries, highlighting the ongoing struggle for self-determination in the face of aggression.

Historical context

THE HISTORICAL CONTEXT surrounding the war mongering against small nations is deeply rooted in power dynamics, where larger nations have often sought to assert their dominance through military and political means. Over centuries, the patterns of aggression against smaller states have revealed a consistent strategy employed by more powerful countries to expand their influence, resources, and territorial control. This strategy has been particularly evident in regions characterised by strategic significance, resource wealth, or geopolitical importance. The consequences have frequently led to a cycle of violence and destabilisation, undermining the sovereignty of smaller nations and impacting their ability to govern effectively.

In the 19th and 20th centuries, several case studies illustrate how imperial ambitions fueled conflicts involving smaller nations. The colonisation of Africa and the Pacific Islands serves as a prime example, as European powers sought to carve up territories, disregarding the existing political structures and cultures. These actions were often justified through a narrative of civilizing missions, yet they primarily aimed to exploit local resources and establish hegemony. Similarly, the Cold War period saw smaller nations caught in the crossfire of superpower rivalry, with the United States and the Soviet Union frequently intervening in local conflicts to advance their ideological agendas, leading to significant loss of life and sovereignty.

Propaganda techniques have been a critical component of war mongering, as larger powers have historically employed narratives that dehumanise and delegitimise smaller nations. Such tactics often portray these nations as threats to regional stability or as incapable of self-governance, creating a justification for intervention. The use of media, cultural narratives, and political rhetoric has enabled larger powers to shape public perception and garner support for aggressive actions. This manipulation of information not only influences domestic audiences but also seeks to sway international opinion, complicating the efforts of smaller nations to assert their rights and sovereignty.

The rise of nationalism in smaller nations has often emerged as a response to external aggression and interference. In many cases, the struggle for self-determination has been fueled by a desire to resist domination, leading to movements that seek to reclaim autonomy and national identity. Historical figures and grassroots movements have played pivotal roles in mobilising support and fostering resilience against external pressures. However, the effectiveness of these movements has varied, often depending on the level of unity among the population and the ability to navigate the complex geopolitical landscape influenced by larger powers.

Strategies for small nations to resist bullying and aggression require a multifaceted approach that encompasses diplomatic, economic, and social dimensions. Building alliances with other small states can enhance collective bargaining power and provide a united front against larger aggressors. Additionally, fostering strong national identities and promoting civic engagement can help galvanize public support for resistance efforts. Engaging in international forums to bring attention to issues of sovereignty and human rights is also crucial, as it can rally global opinion in favor of smaller states. Ultimately, the historical context of war mongering against small nations serves as a reminder of the ongoing struggle for sovereignty, dignity, and justice in the face of overwhelming odds.

Chapter 2: Historical case studies

The invasion of Poland (1939)

The invasion of Poland in September 1939 marked a significant turning point in the landscape of European geopolitics and set the stage for World War II. This aggressive action by Nazi Germany was not merely an act of military expansion; it was a calculated exploitation of Poland's vulnerabilities as a smaller nation facing the encroachment of a larger power. The invasion was characterized by a swift and brutal military campaign known as Blitzkrieg, or "lightning war," which combined rapid assaults by air and ground forces. This approach aimed to overwhelm Polish defenses before they could effectively mobilize, demonstrating the brutal efficiency often employed by aggressors in the face of weaker nations.

The motivations behind the invasion were rooted in both historical grievances and ideological ambitions. Adolf Hitler sought to reclaim territories lost after World War I and to assert Germany's dominance in Central Europe. The Polish Corridor, which granted Poland access to the Baltic Sea, was a particular point of contention for the Nazis, who viewed it as a barrier to their expansionist goals. Propaganda played a crucial role in justifying the invasion, as the German government propagated narratives of a Polish threat, which were largely fabricated to incite public support for military action. This manipulation of public perception is a hallmark of war mongering, often used by larger powers to legitimize aggression against smaller nations.

As Germany invaded from the west, the Soviet Union simultaneously invaded from the east due to the Molotov-Ribbentrop Pact, a non-aggression treaty that included secret protocols for the division of Eastern Europe. This dual invasion further exemplified the precarious position of Poland, which found itself caught between two authoritarian regimes. The lack of effective support from Western allies, particularly Britain and France, who had pledged to defend Poland, highlighted the challenges faced by small nations when larger powers engage in collusion and aggression. The failure of international diplomacy in this context serves as a stark reminder of the difficulties smaller nations encounter in maintaining their sovereignty.

The impact of the invasion extended beyond immediate military concerns; it represented a broader struggle for self-determination in the face of overwhelming odds. Nationalism within Poland surged as citizens rallied to defend their homeland, showcasing the resilience of a small nation against external pressures. However, the subsequent occupation by German and Soviet forces led to severe human rights abuses, including mass executions and the systematic persecution of Polish intellectuals and Jews. This brutal reality underscored the consequences of unchecked aggression, with smaller nations often bearing the brunt of larger powers' ambitions.

In examining the invasion of Poland, it becomes clear that strategies for resisting aggression and war mongering are critical for small nations. Historical case studies reveal the importance of building alliances, fostering international solidarity, and leveraging diplomatic channels to advocate for sovereignty. Additionally, cultivating a strong national identity and preserving cultural heritage can empower smaller nations to stand firm against external threats. The lessons learned from Poland's tragedy in 1939 continue to resonate, serving as a cautionary tale for contemporary issues of aggression against small nations in various parts of the world.

The Vietnam war and its impact on smaller nations

THE VIETNAM WAR, WHICH unfolded from the late 1950s to the mid-1970s, serves as a significant case study in the dynamics of larger powers intervening in the affairs of smaller nations. The conflict did not merely affect Vietnam; its repercussions rippled across Southeast Asia and beyond, influencing the geopolitical landscape and the sovereignty of smaller nations. As the United States escalated its military presence in Vietnam, neighboring countries like Laos and Cambodia became entangled in the conflict. The U.S. bombing campaigns and military operations extended into these nations, which faced the dual pressures of foreign intervention and internal instability.

This situation exemplifies how smaller nations can become pawns in the power struggles of larger states.

The impact of the Vietnam War on smaller nations was profound, as it exacerbated existing tensions and conflicts within these countries. In Cambodia, for instance, the destabilisation caused by U.S. military actions contributed to the rise of the Khmer Rouge, a radical regime that ultimately led to genocide. Laos, often overshadowed in discussions of the Vietnam War, experienced heavy bombings that resulted in significant civilian casualties and a lingering legacy of unexploded ordnance. These occurrences highlight how foreign intervention can undermine the sovereignty of smaller nations, forcing them into conflicts that are not of their making, while also altering their political, social, and economic landscapes.

Moreover, the Vietnam War showcased the use of propaganda techniques by larger powers to justify their interventions in smaller nations. The U.S. government framed its actions as a necessary measure to contain communism and protect democracy, often neglecting the voices of the people in the affected nations. This narrative not only helped garner domestic support for the war but also served to delegitimize the struggles of smaller nations as they sought to assert their sovereignty. The manipulation of public perception through propaganda illustrates a broader pattern wherein larger powers employ similar tactics to rationalize their interventions, often portraying smaller nations as threats that require external intervention to mitigate.

For many in Vietnam, Cambodia, and Laos, resistance to foreign intervention sparked a renewed sense of national identity and unity against perceived imperialist threats. This nationalism was not limited to the battlefield; it also manifested in cultural and political movements that sought to reclaim autonomy and self-determination. The experiences of these nations underscore how foreign aggression can catalyse a resurgence of national pride and solidarity, even in the face of overwhelming odds.

In examining the lessons learned from the Vietnam War, smaller nations today can glean strategies for resisting bullying and aggression from larger powers. Building coalitions with other nations facing similar threats, fostering internal unity through inclusive governance, and leveraging international law and organisations for support are critical steps that can help protect their sovereignty. Furthermore, cultivating a robust national narrative that emphasises self-determination and resilience can empower smaller nations to withstand external pressures. As history has shown, the path toward safeguarding sovereignty is fraught with challenges, yet by learning from past experiences, smaller nations can develop effective strategies to navigate the complexities of international relations in an era still marked by power imbalances.

The Gulf war: Iraq and its neighbours

THE GULF WAR, WHICH erupted in 1990 with Iraq's invasion of Kuwait, serves as a critical case study in the dynamics of war mongering and the implications of foreign intervention on the sovereignty of smaller nations. At the heart of this conflict was Iraq, a nation grappling with its national identity and regional ambitions, particularly under the leadership of Saddam Hussein. The invasion was framed by Iraq as a necessary measure to assert control over its oil-rich neighbor, but it also highlighted the precarious balance of power in the Middle East, where larger states often exert influence over their smaller counterparts. The war not only transformed the geopolitical landscape but also illustrated the vulnerabilities faced by small nations in the face of aggression from more powerful neighbors.

Iraq's relationship with its neighbors was fraught with tension long before the Gulf War. Historically, borders in the region were drawn with little regard for ethnic and tribal affiliations, leading to deep-seated rivalries. Kuwait, once part of the Ottoman Empire and later a British protectorate, became a symbol of Iraq's perceived grievances. The Iraqi government propagated the narrative that Kuwait was an artificial state, created by colonial powers at the expense of Iraq's territorial integrity. This narrative, steeped in nationalism, served as a propaganda tool to justify military action and rally domestic support, showcasing how historical contexts can be manipulated to legitimise aggression against smaller nations.

The response of the international community to Iraq's invasion further underscores the complexities of foreign intervention. The United States, alongside a coalition of allies, launched Operation Desert Storm to liberate Kuwait, framing the intervention as a defense of sovereignty and a stand against aggression. However, this military response also revealed the underlying motivations of larger powers to maintain control over strategic resources, particularly oil. The war illustrated how interventions, while often portrayed as protective measures, can undermine the sovereignty of small nations, leaving them vulnerable to external influences and dictating their political and economic futures.

In the wake of the Gulf War, the aftermath for Iraq and its neighbors was marked by continued instability and conflict. The imposition of sanctions and the subsequent military operations led to significant humanitarian crises, particularly in Iraq, where the civilian population bore the brunt of external pressures. The war also sparked a wave of nationalism among Iraqis, who viewed foreign intervention as an affront to their sovereignty. This rise in nationalism, while a unifying force, also complicated the region's politics, as it gave rise to extremist factions that exploited the chaos. The consequences of the Gulf War thus extended beyond immediate military objectives, reshaping national identities and regional dynamics in profound ways.

The lessons drawn from the Gulf War remain relevant for small nations facing potential aggression from larger powers. Strategies for resisting bullying and maintaining sovereignty are crucial for nations that find themselves in similar predicaments. Diplomatic engagement, forming alliances with other small nations, and leveraging international law can serve as effective tools for countering aggressive actions. Moreover, fostering a strong national identity and promoting resilience among the populace can empower smaller nations to withstand external pressures. Ultimately, the Gulf War exemplifies the intricate interplay between nationalism, foreign intervention, and the vulnerabilities of small nations in a world where power dynamics are often skewed in favor of larger states.

The Balkans conflict: Ethnic tensions and foreign intervention

THE BALKANS CONFLICT, particularly during the 1990s, serves as a poignant example of how ethnic tensions can erupt into violence and how foreign intervention can complicate and exacerbate these conflicts. The dissolution of Yugoslavia revealed deep-seated ethnic rivalries that had been suppressed during the communist regime. As the various republics sought independence, nationalistic fervor surged, leading to brutal confrontations. Ethnic groups such as Serbs, Croats, and Bosniaks found themselves at odds, often fueled by historical grievances, propaganda, and inter-group mistrust, which were manipulated by political leaders to consolidate power and justify aggression.

Foreign intervention played a critical role in shaping the outcome of the Balkans conflict. Initially, the international community's response was tepid, with the United Nations attempting to broker peace while inadequately addressing the humanitarian crisis that unfolded. As atrocities such as ethnic cleansing became widely reported, public outcry mounted, leading to NATO's involvement in 1995. The airstrikes aimed at the Bosnian Serb forces marked a significant shift in foreign policy, illustrating how external powers can influence the trajectory of conflicts in smaller nations. However, this intervention was not without controversy, as it raised questions about sovereignty and the implications of foreign military presence in domestic disputes.

The impact of foreign intervention on the sovereignty of small nations is a crucial consideration in the study of the Balkans conflict. While the military assistance provided by NATO ultimately helped to end the violence in Bosnia, it also established a precedent for outside powers to intervene in the internal affairs of sovereign states under the guise of humanitarian intervention. This duality complicates the narrative of liberation versus domination, as small nations may find their national interests overshadowed by the agendas of larger powers. The long-term consequences of such interventions can lead to a dependency on foreign support, undermining the ability of these nations to chart their own political futures.

Propaganda played an instrumental role in the Balkans conflict, as various factions employed media to shape public perception and galvanise support for their causes. Nationalist leaders used propaganda techniques to dehumanise opposing ethnic groups and justify their actions, creating an environment ripe for conflict. This manipulation of information not only fueled violence but also influenced the international community's response. The portrayal of victims and aggressors became a powerful tool in garnering sympathy and support, highlighting how narratives can be crafted to serve the interests of those wielding power, often at the expense of the truth.

In the wake of the Balkans conflict, small nations facing aggression must develop strategies to resist bullying and external manipulation. Emphasising unity among diverse ethnic groups, fostering dialogue, and promoting a strong civil society can empower nations to navigate the complexities of foreign intervention and maintain their sovereignty. Additionally, leveraging international law and alliances can provide a framework for support against aggression. The lessons learned from the Balkans demonstrate the need for small nations to remain vigilant against the forces of nationalism and external influence, ensuring that their voices and interests are not overshadowed by the ambitions of larger powers.

Chapter 3: The impact of foreign intervention

Sovereignty vs. Intervention

Sovereignty and intervention present a complex dichotomy in the context of international relations, particularly for small nations that often find themselves vulnerable to larger powers. Sovereignty refers to the authority of a state to govern itself without external interference, a principle enshrined in international law. However, this ideal is frequently challenged by the actions of more powerful nations that justify intervention under various pretexts, such as humanitarian concerns, national security, or the promotion of democracy. This subchapter explores the tension between these two concepts, examining how larger powers manipulate the notion of intervention to undermine the sovereignty of weaker states.

Historical case studies illustrate the recurring theme of war mongering against small nations. One notable example is the U.S. intervention in Grenada in 1983, which was framed as a mission to restore democracy and protect American citizens. However, this intervention reflected broader geopolitical interests rather than genuine humanitarian concerns. Similarly, the NATO bombing of Yugoslavia in the late 1990s was justified on the grounds of protecting ethnic Albanians but raised significant questions about the sovereignty of the Federal Republic of Yugoslavia. These cases underscore how the rhetoric of intervention can be employed to legitimize actions that fundamentally challenge the autonomy of targeted nations.

When a foreign power intervenes, it can lead to a loss of control over national affairs, as external actors may impose their political or economic agendas. This can result in destabilisation, social unrest, and long-term dependency on foreign aid or military support. For instance, the intervention in Libya in 2011, initially seen as a means to prevent humanitarian disaster, ultimately led to civil war and ongoing conflict, undermining the country's sovereignty and leaving its future uncertain. Such outcomes highlight the precarious position of small nations caught in the crossfire of larger geopolitical struggles.

Propaganda techniques play a crucial role in the narrative surrounding interventions, often painting the targeted nation as a threat or a victim in need of external assistance. This manipulation of public perception can rally domestic and international support for intervention, masking the underlying motivations driven by power dynamics and resource control. For example, the portrayal of Iraq in the lead-up to the 2003 invasion relied heavily on claims of weapons of mass destruction and links to terrorism, which were later discredited. This illustrates how propaganda not only justifies intervention but also fosters an environment where the sovereignty of small nations is disregarded in favor of larger strategic interests.

In the face of aggression and intervention, small nations have employed various strategies to resist bullying and maintain their sovereignty. Building strong diplomatic ties with other nations, participating in international organisations, and fostering a sense of nationalism are essential components of a robust defense against external pressures. Additionally, small nations can leverage their unique cultural heritages and identities to garner international sympathy and support. By promoting narratives that highlight their sovereignty and resilience, these nations can challenge the prevailing discourse that often sidelines their rights and autonomy. Through these strategies, small nations can assert their independence even in the face of overwhelming odds, reflecting the enduring struggle for sovereignty amidst the realities of global power dynamics.

Economic consequences for small nations

WHEN LARGER POWERS engage in aggressive tactics against these smaller states, the immediate impact often manifests in severe disruptions to their economies. Small nations, typically reliant on a limited range of industries and exports, find their economic stability threatened. This can lead to significant drops in GDP, increased unemployment, and the loss of essential services.

DISSUADING WAR MONGERS

The economic turmoil can further exacerbate existing vulnerabilities, making it difficult for these nations to recover even after hostilities cease.

In many cases, the imposition of sanctions or trade embargoes by more powerful nations serves as a tool of economic warfare. These measures can cripple small nations by cutting them off from essential goods and markets. For instance, countries that rely on agriculture may find their exports heavily restricted, resulting in excess production and subsequent financial losses. Additionally, the freezing of financial assets and restrictions on international banking can deter foreign investment, leading to a vicious cycle of economic decline and isolation. The long-term ramifications can stifle growth and hinder development, forcing small nations into a precarious position.

Small nations often experience a decline in consumer confidence, leading to decreased spending and investment within their borders. The fear of instability can prompt citizens to move abroad in search of better opportunities, draining the nation of its human capital. This exodus can create a brain drain that further limits the economic potential of these countries. As the demographics shift, the remaining population may face increased pressures on social services, compounding the challenges of recovery.

The role of foreign intervention also complicates the economic landscape for small nations. In some instances, external powers may exploit the vulnerabilities of these nations, imposing conditions that favor foreign interests rather than local development. This can lead to the establishment of monopolies or the extraction of resources without fair compensation, undermining the sovereignty and economic autonomy of the small nation. Such interventions can create dependencies that are difficult to break, as local governments may find themselves beholden to foreign powers for economic survival.

Despite these challenges, small nations have developed various strategies to resist economic bullying. Many focus on building strong domestic institutions and diversifying their economies to reduce vulnerability to external pressures. Additionally, fostering regional cooperation can enhance collective bargaining power against larger nations. By promoting nationalism and a sense of unity, small nations can galvanise their populations to support policies that prioritise local interests over foreign demands. Ultimately, the resilience of small nations in the face of economic aggression lies in their ability to adapt and assert their sovereignty against the tide of war mongering.

Political ramifications of intervention

THE POLITICAL RAMIFICATIONS of intervention in small nations are profoundly disruptive because they are often reshaping the geopolitical landscape in ways that extend far beyond immediate military outcomes. When larger powers intervene in the affairs of smaller nations, the primary political consequence is the erosion of sovereignty. This loss can manifest in various forms, including diminished self-governance, altered political structures, and the imposition of foreign ideologies. The smaller nation may find itself caught in a web of alliances and dependencies, complicating its ability to make autonomous decisions. This shift can lead to long-term instability, as the local populace grapples with the repercussions of foreign control and the loss of national identity.

The intervention often breeds resentment and resistance among the local population, leading to a rise in nationalism. In many cases, the aggressive actions of larger powers ignite a sense of unity among citizens of the targeted nation, reinforcing their collective identity against perceived external threats. This nationalism can be a double-edged sword; while it may galvanise the public to resist foreign influence, it can also lead to internal divisions if different factions emerge with competing visions for the nation's future. The political landscape becomes a battleground for competing ideologies, complicating efforts to establish a cohesive national front.

Moreover, foreign intervention frequently alters the balance of power within a region. Larger powers may use small nations as pawns in broader geopolitical strategies, creating a landscape where local conflicts are exacerbated by external involvement. Such interventions can lead to proxy wars, where smaller nations become arenas for larger powers to exert influence without engaging directly in conflict. Consequently, the political ramifications extend beyond the immediate area, affecting regional stability and international relations. The involvement of multiple foreign actors can create a complex interplay of allegiances and hostilities, making conflict resolution increasingly difficult.

Larger powers often employ sophisticated propaganda techniques to justify their interventions and sway public opinion, both domestically and internationally. By framing their actions as benevolent or necessary for global stability, these powers obscure the detrimental effects of their interventions on small nations' sovereignty. This manipulation of narratives can undermine the legitimacy of local governments and foster divisions among the populace, further complicating the political situation. Propaganda serves not only as a tool for justifying intervention but also as a means of controlling the narrative surrounding the aftermath, shaping perceptions long after the military presence has withdrawn.

Ultimately, small nations facing aggression must navigate these complex political ramifications with strategic foresight. Developing robust diplomatic relations, fostering regional alliances, and engaging in grassroots movements can empower these nations to resist foreign bullying and assert their sovereignty. It is essential for small nations to cultivate a strong sense of national identity and unity among their citizens, as this can serve as a powerful counter to external pressures. By prioritising these strategies, small nations can not only survive attempts at intervention but potentially emerge stronger, more resilient, and more capable of asserting their independence in an increasingly volatile global landscape.

Media manipulation and disinformation

MEDIA MANIPULATION and disinformation have become pivotal strategies in the arsenal of larger powers engaging in war mongering against smaller nations. These tactics are employed to shape public perception, create narratives that justify aggressive actions, and undermine the sovereignty of targeted states. By controlling the information landscape, powerful nations can effectively distort the reality of conflicts and influence both domestic and international opinion. This manipulation often involves the use of selective reporting, propaganda, and the dissemination of false information, which together create a distorted view of the situation on the ground.

In historical case studies, we observe how media manipulation has played a crucial role in framing conflicts. For instance, during the lead-up to the Gulf War in the early 1990s, reports of atrocities committed by Iraqi forces in Kuwait were amplified through various media channels. These accounts, many of which were later proven to be exaggerated or fabricated, helped to galvanise public support for military intervention. By crafting a narrative of moral righteousness, the media allowed for a swift military response that disregarded the sovereignty of Iraq, demonstrating how disinformation can set the stage for war.

When larger powers engage in military action, they frequently justify their interventions through manipulated media narratives that portray the targeted nation as a threat or as a failed state. This not only leads to the erosion of the targeted nation's autonomy but also stifles its ability to respond effectively to external aggression. The psychological toll on the populace, compounded by the feeling of being misrepresented in global discourse, can further weaken national resolve and unity against foreign interventions.

Propaganda techniques are integral to the bullying of small nations, as they serve to dehumanise the adversary and rally support for aggressive policies. Techniques such as creating fear through sensationalism, employing emotional appeals, and using misinformation to evoke outrage can effectively sway public opinion. By leveraging these methods, larger powers can foster a narrative that casts their actions as defensive rather than aggressive, thus framing the conflict in a way that diminishes accountability and justifies their larger geopolitical ambitions.

As nationalism rises in small nations facing aggression, it can serve as both a shield and a weapon against external manipulation. A strong sense of national identity can empower citizens to recognise and challenge disinformation campaigns aimed at undermining their sovereignty. By fostering media literacy and encouraging critical engagement with information, small nations can develop strategies to resist bullying and aggression. Furthermore, forming alliances with other nations facing similar threats can enhance resilience against the tactics of larger powers, ensuring that the voices of smaller nations are not drowned out by the clamor of more dominant narratives.

The role of social media in modern warfare

THE ROLE OF SOCIAL media in modern warfare has transformed the landscape of conflict, particularly in how larger powers engage with smaller nations. In an era where information spreads rapidly and globally, social media platforms serve as both a battlefield and a tool for propaganda. Governments and non-state actors alike harness these platforms to shape narratives, influence public perception, and mobilize support for their agendas. For smaller nations, this presents a dual challenge: not only must they contend with traditional military threats, but they also face a barrage of information warfare that seeks to undermine their sovereignty and legitimacy.

One of the primary functions of social media in modern warfare is the dissemination of propaganda. Larger powers often exploit these platforms to create and spread disinformation aimed at discrediting smaller nations. This can take the form of manipulated images, misleading statistics, or outright false narratives that paint the targeted nation in a negative light. For instance, during conflicts in regions like Eastern Europe and the Middle East, social media has been used to amplify claims about governmental incompetence or human rights abuses, thereby justifying foreign intervention or aggression. This manipulation of information can erode public trust in the leadership of smaller nations, making it easier for larger powers to exert influence.

Moreover, social media acts as a tool for mobilization and recruitment. Armed groups and state actors can use these platforms to rally support for their causes, often framing their actions as necessary responses to perceived threats from smaller nations. Campaigns on social media can quickly galvanize public opinion, both domestically and internationally, leading to an escalation of tensions. Smaller nations, struggling to counter these narratives, often find themselves outmatched in the digital arena, where the speed and reach of information can outpace their efforts to respond. This imbalance can have dire consequences, as public sentiment sways in favor of intervention based on distorted information.

In addition to propaganda and mobilisation, social media provides a means for smaller nations to share their perspectives and counteract the narratives pushed by larger powers. By utilising these platforms effectively, smaller nations can engage directly with global audiences, presenting their side of the story and highlighting the implications of foreign aggression. This engagement can foster international solidarity, drawing attention to their plight and potentially influencing foreign governments and organisations to reconsider their positions. However, the effectiveness of this strategy relies heavily on the ability of these nations to navigate the complexities of social media, including algorithmic biases and the dominance of larger, more established voices.

Ultimately, the role of social media in modern warfare underscores the importance of digital literacy and strategic communication for smaller nations facing aggression. As they confront the realities of both military threats and information warfare, these nations must develop comprehensive strategies to protect their sovereignty and promote their narratives. This includes not only enhancing their own social media presence but also collaborating with allies and organisations committed to defending democratic values and sovereignty. In a world where information is a powerful weapon, the ability to wield it effectively can be as crucial as any traditional military capability.

Historical examples of propaganda against small nations

THE HISTORICAL LANDSCAPE is replete with examples of propaganda used against small nations, often as a precursor or justification for larger powers to exert control or influence. One notable instance is the lead-up to the American invasion of Iraq in 2003, where the U.S. government utilised a coordinated media campaign to portray the Iraqi regime as a significant threat to global security. This campaign included the dissemination of exaggerated claims about weapons of mass destruction and ties to terrorist organisations, which ultimately served to manipulate public perception and build support for military intervention. Such tactics underscore how propaganda can distort reality and create a narrative that vilifies smaller nations, facilitating their subjugation.

Another historical example can be found in the treatment of the Baltic states during the Soviet era. The USSR employed extensive propaganda to depict the Baltic nations—Estonia, Latvia, and Lithuania—as integral parts of the Soviet Union, promoting the idea that their independence was a threat to stability. This narrative was reinforced through cultural and educational initiatives that sought to erase national identities and promote a Soviet identity instead. The use of propaganda in this context not only justified military occupation but also aimed to delegitimize the sovereignty of these nations, contributing to their struggles for independence that would only gain momentum decades later.

The case of the Rwandan genocide in 1994 further illustrates the role of propaganda in undermining small nations. Leading up to the atrocities, the Hutu-led government utilised state-controlled media to spread anti-Tutsi rhetoric, portraying them as the enemy and a threat to Hutu survival. This systematic dehumanisation created an environment in which violence was not only accepted but encouraged. The international community's failure to intervene effectively during this time highlights how propaganda can foster an atmosphere of impunity for aggressors while marginalising the voices of innocent civilians in small nations.

In the context of the former Yugoslavia, the Bosnian War serves as a poignant example of how propaganda was employed to justify ethnic cleansing against Bosniaks and Croats. Serbian nationalists used propaganda to craft a narrative of historical grievances and existential threats, framing their violent actions as a necessary defense of the Serbian people. This manipulation of historical memory and identity not only rallied support for aggressive military actions but also obscured the humanitarian crisis unfolding in the region. It reveals the profound impact of propaganda in shaping perceptions and justifying violence against smaller groups within larger national conflicts.

Finally, the ongoing situation in Ukraine illustrates how propaganda continues to be a potent weapon against smaller nations facing aggression from larger powers. The Russian government has employed various propaganda strategies to frame its actions in Ukraine as protective measures for ethnic Russians, while simultaneously discrediting the Ukrainian government as illegitimate. This narrative has been amplified through state-controlled media and social platforms, influencing public opinion both domestically and internationally. The case of Ukraine exemplifies the significant role propaganda plays in contemporary conflicts, demonstrating that the principles of war mongering against small nations are not relics of the past but remain relevant in current geopolitical dynamics.

Chapter 4: Profiles of targeted small nations

The Baltic States: Estonia, Latvia, and Lithuania

The Baltic States—Estonia, Latvia, and Lithuania—exemplify the complex interplay of nationalism, foreign intervention, and war mongering against smaller nations. Situated on the eastern edge of Europe, these countries have faced significant external pressures throughout their histories, particularly from larger powers seeking to expand their influence. The legacy of foreign domination, notably during the Soviet era, has shaped their national identities and political landscapes. The Baltic States emerged from the shadow of the USSR in the early 1990s, and their subsequent paths toward sovereignty and integration into Western institutions highlight the challenges faced by small nations in the face of aggression.

Historically, the Baltic States have been caught between competing imperial ambitions, notably those of Russia and Germany. The three countries declared independence after World War I but were subsequently occupied and annexed by the Soviet Union in 1940. This occupation was marked by repression, forced collectivisation, and the suppression of national identities. The resilience of the Baltic peoples during this time is noteworthy; they preserved their cultures and languages in the face of systematic efforts to eradicate them. The struggle for independence in the late 1980s, exemplified by mass movements such as the Singing Revolution, showcased the power of nationalism in resisting external domination.

The role of foreign intervention has been pivotal in the Baltic States' pursuit of sovereignty. The support of Western nations during the Cold War, particularly through propaganda and diplomatic channels, provided a lifeline for these nations. Post-1991, NATO and the European Union expanded to include Estonia, Latvia, and Lithuania, offering not just military protection but also a framework for economic and political stability. Nevertheless, the presence of larger powers, especially Russia, continues to loom over the region, with ongoing military exercises and cyber threats that challenge the sovereignty of these small nations.

Propaganda techniques have also played a crucial role in the narratives surrounding the Baltic States. Russia has employed disinformation campaigns to undermine public confidence in their governments and to foster divisions along ethnic lines. This strategy aims to destabilize these nations from within, portraying them as weak and incapable of self-governance. The Baltic governments, in turn, have countered these narratives through strategic communication efforts, emphasizing their democratic values and commitment to human rights while fostering a strong sense of national identity and unity among their populations.

In conclusion, the experiences of Estonia, Latvia, and Lithuania serve as a case study of how small nations can navigate the treacherous waters of international politics marked by war mongering and aggression. Their historical struggles have instilled resilience and a strong sense of nationalism that continue to inform their strategies against external pressures. As these nations face ongoing challenges, including the rise of populism and external threats, their ability to maintain sovereignty and promote a cohesive national identity will be critical in resisting aggression and ensuring their place in the international community.

Central American nations: Guatemala and Nicaragua

CENTRAL AMERICAN NATIONS, particularly Guatemala and Nicaragua, have faced significant challenges from larger powers throughout their histories, often under the guise of political or ideological intervention. These two nations exemplify how regional dynamics, fueled by foreign interests, can lead to a cycle of instability and conflict. The historical context of U.S. involvement in these countries reveals a pattern of war mongering that has undermined their sovereignty and exacerbated internal strife. The case of Guatemala, particularly during the 1950s, illustrates how the fear of communism was leveraged to justify interventions that ultimately served corporate interests rather than the welfare of the local population.

In Guatemala, the CIA orchestrated a coup in 1954 to overthrow President Jacobo Árbenz, who had initiated land reforms that threatened the interests of the United Fruit Company. This intervention was framed as a necessary action to prevent the spread of communism in Central America, but it resulted in decades of civil war and human rights abuses. The narrative constructed by U.S. policymakers portrayed Árbenz as a communist sympathizer, using propaganda techniques that painted a simplistic dichotomy of good versus evil. As a result, the Guatemalan people suffered long-term consequences, including a legacy of violence and political instability driven by external manipulation.

Nicaragua's experience in the 1980s further exemplifies the detrimental effects of foreign intervention on small nations. Following the Sandinista revolution, which overthrew the Somoza dictatorship, the U.S. government sought to destabilise the new regime by supporting the Contras, a rebel group that engaged in a brutal campaign against the Sandinista government. The U.S. portrayed the Sandinistas as a communist threat, employing a range of propaganda techniques to rally domestic and international support for its intervention. This conflict not only led to widespread suffering and displacement within Nicaragua but also highlighted the broader implications of foreign meddling in the sovereignty of nations that dare to chart their own political paths.

The influence of nationalism in both Guatemala and Nicaragua has been a crucial factor in their responses to foreign aggression. In Guatemala, the push for land reform and social justice galvanised various indigenous and leftist movements, fostering a sense of national identity that resisted external pressures. Similarly, Nicaragua's Sandinista revolution was rooted in a deep-seated desire for sovereignty and self-determination, which enabled the populace to unify against foreign-funded insurgents. These nationalist sentiments have often served as a double-edged sword, providing both a rallying point for resistance and a target for foreign powers seeking to exploit divisions within the countries.

Strategies for small nations like Guatemala and Nicaragua to resist bullying and aggression involve fostering strong national identities, building regional alliances, and advocating for international support through diplomatic channels. By promoting economic independence and social cohesion, these nations can mitigate the vulnerabilities that make them targets for larger powers. Moreover, engaging in collective regional initiatives can enhance their bargaining power on the global stage, allowing them to confront external pressures more effectively. As the histories of Guatemala and Nicaragua illustrate, the struggle against war mongering is not solely about military might but also about the resilience of national identity and the capacity to mobilize against foreign domination.

The Caribbean: Cuba and Haiti

THE CARIBBEAN REGION has long been a focal point for geopolitical interests, particularly in the cases of Cuba and Haiti. Both nations have experienced significant external pressures and interventions that have shaped their political landscapes and national identities. Cuba, with its strategic location and revolutionary history, became a target for U.S. interventionist policies throughout the 20th century. Similarly, Haiti, the first independent nation in Latin America and the Caribbean, has faced a series of foreign interventions that have undermined its sovereignty and stability, revealing patterns of war mongering by more powerful nations.

Cuba's defiance against U.S. hegemony began with the 1959 revolution led by Fidel Castro, which aimed to eradicate colonial influences and establish socialist principles. The U.S. response included economic sanctions, the Bay of Pigs invasion, and a series of covert operations aimed at destabilizing the Cuban government. These actions showcased a willingness to use military force and propaganda to maintain control over the Caribbean and prevent the spread of communism. The narrative constructed around Cuba was often framed in terms of national security, depicting the island as a significant threat to regional stability, which justified aggressive policies against it.

Haiti's history of foreign intervention is marked by both U.S. military occupations and economic manipulation. The U.S. occupied Haiti from 1915 to 1934, ostensibly to restore order and protect American interests. However, this occupation resulted in the erosion of Haitian sovereignty and the establishment of a system that favored foreign businesses at the expense of local development. The subsequent political instability and economic challenges faced by Haiti can be traced back to these interventions, which often left the nation vulnerable to external exploitation and internal strife. The narrative surrounding Haiti has frequently been one of chaos and instability, which has been used to justify ongoing interventions and the imposition of foreign governance.

Propaganda techniques have played a crucial role in shaping perceptions of both Cuba and Haiti, often portraying them as failed states that require external assistance. This narrative serves to legitimise intervention while obscuring the historical context of foreign exploitation and interference. In the case of Cuba, the U.S. has used media portrayals to depict the government as oppressive and authoritarian, ignoring the social advancements made since the revolution. For Haiti, the portrayal often emphasises poverty and disorder, which distracts from the impact of historical injustices and foreign interventions that have contributed to its challenges.

Nationalism has emerged as a critical response to foreign aggression in both Cuba and Haiti. In Cuba, national pride and a commitment to sovereignty have fueled resistance to U.S. influence, inspiring a strong sense of identity rooted in the revolutionary struggle. Similarly, in Haiti, efforts to reclaim sovereignty and dignity have been manifested through grassroots movements and calls for self-determination. These nationalist sentiments not only empower citizens to resist external pressures but also foster a collective identity that is essential for navigating the complexities of international relations in a world often dominated by larger powers.

The South Pacific: Fiji and the Solomon Islands

THE SOUTH PACIFIC HAS long been a region where the interplay of power dynamics is starkly visible, particularly in the cases of Fiji and the Solomon Islands. Both nations, characterised by their strategic locations and rich resources, have found themselves vulnerable to the interests of larger powers. The geopolitical significance of these islands has often made them targets for foreign interventions, which, while often framed as aid or support, can lead to substantial infringements on their sovereignty. The historical context surrounding these interventions reveals a pattern of war mongering that exploits the weaknesses of small nations.

Fiji has experienced several coups and political instabilities since its independence in 1970, often influenced by external actors. The geopolitical interests of countries like Australia and New Zealand have manifested in various forms of intervention, sometimes justified by the need to restore democracy or stability. However, these interventions have often resulted in a loss of local autonomy and an increased presence of foreign military and economic interests. The narrative crafted around these interventions frequently employs propaganda techniques that depict local leaders as incapable, thereby justifying external oversight and control.

Similarly, the Solomon Islands have been a focal point of foreign intervention, particularly during the civil unrest in the early 2000s. The Australian-led Regional Assistance Mission to Solomon Islands (RAMSI) was initiated under the pretext of restoring order. While RAMSI succeeded in stabilising the country, it also highlighted the complexities of foreign involvement. The mission's long-term effects on national sovereignty and local governance raise questions about the genuine intentions behind such interventions. The portrayal of local conflicts in the media often simplifies the issues, casting foreign powers as benevolent saviors rather than recognising their role in exacerbating tensions.

The influence of nationalism in both Fiji and the Solomon Islands cannot be understated, as it plays a crucial role in shaping responses to aggression and intervention. Nationalist sentiments often arise in direct response to perceived threats to sovereignty, prompting movements that seek to reclaim local governance and resist foreign influence. In Fiji, nationalist rhetoric has been used to unite various ethnic groups against external pressures, while in the Solomon Islands, local leaders have increasingly called for a reassertion of control over their resources and political systems. These movements reflect a broader trend among small nations to resist the narrative imposed by larger powers and reclaim their agency.

For small nations like Fiji and the Solomon Islands, developing strategies to counteract foreign bullying and aggression is essential for maintaining sovereignty. Building strong national identities, fostering regional cooperation, and engaging in diplomatic channels are crucial steps in this process. By strengthening their internal governance and asserting their rights on the international stage, these nations can resist the pressures that come from larger powers. Ultimately, the experiences of Fiji and the Solomon Islands serve as critical case studies in understanding the dynamics of war mongering and the resilience of small nations in the face of external threats.

Chapter 5: Nationalism and its influence

National identity in the face of aggression

National identity plays a crucial role in the resilience of small nations facing aggression. When external forces threaten their sovereignty, these nations often rally around a shared sense of history, culture, and purpose. This collective identity becomes a bulwark against the pressures of larger powers that seek to undermine their autonomy. The formation of national identity is deeply intertwined with the experiences of oppression and resistance, leading to a strengthened resolve among the populace to defend their rights and heritage. This dynamic is especially evident in regions where historical grievances have shaped collective memory, fostering a spirit of unity in the face of aggression.

Throughout history, many small nations have experienced the detrimental effects of war mongering, where larger states exploit geopolitical tensions to exert control. In these instances, the national identity of the smaller nation often serves as a counterweight to the aggressor's narrative. For example, during conflicts, dominant powers frequently employ propaganda techniques that distort the reality of the situation, aiming to delegitimise the small nation's claims to sovereignty. However, a robust national identity can challenge these narratives, as citizens draw on their unique cultural and historical contexts to assert their legitimacy and resist subjugation. This interplay between identity and aggression highlights the importance of understanding how these nations construct their self-image amid external threats.

The influence of nationalism in small nations under siege cannot be overstated. Nationalism can galvanise public sentiment, inspiring citizens to engage in collective action against aggressors. In many cases, the resurgence of national pride has prompted grassroots movements that advocate for self-determination and resistance to foreign intervention. This sense of nationalism can transform into a powerful tool for mobilization, enabling small nations to unite disparate groups under a common cause. The articulation of national identity becomes an essential strategy for fostering solidarity and resilience, allowing these nations to navigate the complexities of international relations with a sense of purpose and agency.

Strategies for small nations to resist bullying and aggression often hinge on the cultivation of a strong national identity. By emphasizing their unique cultural attributes, historical narratives, and shared values, these nations can create a narrative that resonates both domestically and internationally. Diplomatic efforts to garner support from allies can be fortified by showcasing the strength of their national identity, framing their struggles as part of a broader fight for self-determination. Additionally, leveraging international platforms to highlight their plight can amplify their voices, drawing attention to the injustices they face and fostering a sense of solidarity among like-minded nations.

Role of nationalism in resistance movements

NATIONALISM PLAYS A crucial role in the resistance movements of small nations facing aggression from larger powers. It serves as a unifying force that fosters a collective identity among the citizens, emphasizing shared history, culture, and aspirations. When external threats loom, this sense of nationalism can galvanise the populace, mobilising them to defend their sovereignty and promote their interests. Leaders of resistance movements often harness this sentiment to rally support, framing the struggle as a fight for national dignity and self-determination.

Historically, nationalism has been a powerful motivator in various case studies of small nations resisting foreign intervention. In the face of colonial domination or imperial expansion, nationalist movements have emerged as significant responses. For instance, during the decolonization period in the mid-20th century, many nations in Africa and Asia adopted nationalist rhetoric to challenge the legitimacy of colonial rule. This emphasis on national identity not only inspired local populations but also attracted international attention and sympathy, thereby increasing pressure on colonial powers to relinquish control.

Moreover, the impact of nationalism is often amplified by the presence of foreign intervention. When larger powers impose their will on small nations, the reaction is frequently a surge in nationalist sentiment. The invasion of Iraq in 2003, for example, prompted widespread anti-occupation movements fueled by a renewed sense of Iraqi identity and nationalism. Communities that may have been divided along ethnic or sectarian lines found common ground in their opposition to foreign military presence, illustrating how external aggression can solidify national unity in the face of adversity.

In addition to fostering unity, nationalism can also serve as a strategic tool for small nations seeking to resist aggression. By framing their struggles in terms of national survival and identity, these nations can effectively counteract propaganda used by larger powers that often seeks to dehumanize or delegitimize their cause. Nationalist narratives can highlight the historical injustices faced by the nation, thereby appealing to both domestic and international audiences. This strategic use of nationalism not only seeks to garner support but also aims to reinforce the moral high ground of the resistance movement.

Finally, the influence of nationalism in resistance movements underscores the importance of fostering a strong national identity among citizens of small nations. Education, cultural preservation, and the promotion of national symbols can empower individuals and communities to resist external pressures and assert their rights. By cultivating a sense of pride and belonging, small nations can create resilient societies capable of standing firm against bullying and aggression from larger powers. Ultimately, the role of nationalism in these contexts is not merely about resistance, but also about the enduring quest for autonomy and the affirmation of national identity in an increasingly complex global landscape.

Case studies of successful nationalist movements

IN EXAMINING THE DYNAMICS of nationalism in the context of foreign aggression, several case studies emerge that exemplify successful nationalist movements against larger powers. The emergence of these movements often stems from a combination of cultural identity, historical grievances, and a desire for self-determination. One notable example is the struggle for independence by India from British colonial rule. The Indian National Congress, alongside figures like Mahatma Gandhi, effectively mobilized mass support through nonviolent resistance and civil disobedience, ultimately leading to India's independence in 1947. This case illustrates how a cohesive nationalist movement can leverage both cultural solidarity and strategic nonviolent tactics to overcome imperial domination.

Another significant case is the rise of nationalism in Vietnam during the mid-20th century, where the Viet Minh, led by Ho Chi Minh, fought against French colonial rule and later against American intervention. The movement was characterized by a deep-rooted sense of national identity and resilience against foreign powers. The Viet Minh employed guerrilla tactics, garnered support from the peasantry, and utilized international sympathy to highlight their cause. Their eventual victory in the Vietnam War serves as a testament to the effectiveness of a unified nationalist movement in resisting external aggression and asserting sovereignty.

The dissolution of the Soviet Union in the early 1990s offers a different perspective on successful nationalist movements. Several republics, such as the Baltic states of Estonia, Latvia, and Lithuania, capitalized on the waning influence of Moscow to assert their independence. These nations utilized a combination of peaceful protests, cultural revival, and international advocacy to garner support for their sovereignty. The "Singing Revolution" in Estonia exemplifies how cultural expressions, such as music and public gatherings, can galvanize a population towards national unity and independence, ultimately leading to the restoration of their sovereignty in 1991.

In the context of Africa, the case of Eritrea's struggle for independence from Ethiopia showcases the role of a nationalist movement in resisting aggression and colonial legacies. The Eritrean War of Independence, which lasted from 1961 to 1991, was marked by a protracted armed struggle led by the Eritrean People's Liberation Front (EPLF). This movement combined military resistance with grassroots mobilisation, emphasizing the importance of national identity and the right to self-determination. Eritrea's eventual independence highlights how sustained efforts and a clear nationalist agenda can lead to the successful assertion of sovereignty in the face of larger adversarial forces.

These case studies collectively illustrate that successful nationalist movements against larger powers often involve a blend of cultural identity, strategic resistance, and international advocacy. The effectiveness of these movements is amplified when they foster a strong sense of national unity and purpose among their populations. Furthermore, the lessons learned from these historical examples underscore the potential for smaller nations to resist foreign intervention and assert their sovereignty, even when faced with seemingly insurmountable odds. In a world where war mongering and bullying of small nations persist, these case studies serve as a source of inspiration and strategic insight for contemporary movements seeking to navigate similar challenges.

Chapter 6: Strategies for resistance

Building diplomatic alliances is a crucial strategy for small nations facing the threat of war mongering and aggression from larger powers. Throughout history, smaller states have often found themselves at a disadvantage due to their limited military capabilities and economic resources. As a response, many have sought to forge alliances with other nations to enhance their security and assert their sovereignty. These alliances can take various forms, including formal treaties, regional coalitions, and informal partnerships that allow smaller nations to combine their efforts against common threats.

One of the most effective ways for small nations to build diplomatic alliances is through regional cooperation. By collaborating with neighboring countries that share similar interests and vulnerabilities, smaller states can create a united front against potential aggressors. For instance, the Baltic States—Estonia, Latvia, and Lithuania—have effectively strengthened their collective security by working closely with each other and engaging with larger powers like NATO. Such regional alliances not only enhance military capabilities but also foster economic collaboration and cultural exchange, further solidifying ties between nations.

Another significant avenue for building diplomatic alliances is through international organisations. Small nations can leverage platforms such as the United Nations, the African Union, or the Association of Southeast Asian Nations to gain visibility and support for their causes. By participating in these organisations, smaller states can advocate for their sovereignty and highlight the threats they face from larger powers. Additionally, these platforms provide opportunities for smaller nations to form coalitions with like-minded countries, amplifying their voices on the global stage and increasing their bargaining power.

Small nations can employ cultural diplomacy, economic partnerships, and humanitarian initiatives to foster goodwill and strengthen relationships with other countries. By promoting their unique cultural identities and values, smaller states can attract allies who are sympathetic to their plight and are willing to support their sovereignty. For example, nations like Bhutan and Costa Rica have effectively used their commitment to environmental sustainability and peace to build strong diplomatic ties with various global partners, thereby gaining allies in their quest for security.

Finally, the establishment of strategic partnerships with influential global powers can provide small nations with the necessary leverage to resist aggression. By aligning themselves with larger states that have vested interests in their stability and security, smaller nations can enhance their deterrence capabilities. Such partnerships often come with military aid, economic support, and political backing, which can be pivotal in countering the threats posed by war mongering. However, small nations must navigate these relationships carefully, ensuring that they do not compromise their sovereignty or become overly dependent on their allies, thereby maintaining a balance between collaboration and autonomy in the international arena.

Economic self-sufficiency

ECONOMIC SELF-SUFFICIENCY is a critical factor for small nations facing war mongering and external aggression. When a nation can sustain its economy independently, it reduces its vulnerability to external pressures and manipulation. Economic self-sufficiency involves cultivating domestic industries, ensuring food security, and fostering local enterprises that can withstand global market fluctuations. For small nations, the ability to produce essential goods and services not only enhances their resilience but also empowers them to assert their sovereignty in the face of bullying from larger powers.

Historically, many small nations have been targeted for their resources, strategic locations, or geopolitical significance. The lack of economic self-sufficiency in these nations often leads to dependency on foreign aid, trade, and investment, making them susceptible to exploitation. For example, the economic strategies imposed by larger nations can create a cycle of dependency that leaves small nations with limited autonomy. By prioritising economic self-sufficiency through diversified production and local resource management, small nations can mitigate the risks associated with foreign intervention and interference.

Nationalism plays a significant role in fostering economic self-sufficiency among small nations. A strong sense of national identity can motivate citizens to support local industries and prioritise domestic products over foreign imports. This cultural shift not only strengthens the economy but also bolsters national pride and unity in the face of external threats. By promoting the narrative that self-reliance is synonymous with sovereignty, small nations can cultivate a proactive approach to their economic policies, reinforcing their resistance against war mongering and external manipulation.

Moreover, the implementation of strategic policies aimed at enhancing economic self-sufficiency is essential for small nations to counter aggression. Investment in education, technology, and infrastructure can lay the foundation for sustainable economic growth. Encouraging innovation and entrepreneurship within local communities can also foster resilience against external economic pressures. By developing robust economic systems that prioritise local needs and capabilities, small nations can create an environment less susceptible to the whims of larger powers and their aggressive tactics.

Finally, the path to economic self-sufficiency requires collaboration among small nations. By forming alliances and trade agreements with like-minded countries, they can share resources, knowledge, and strategies for economic independence. Collective action not only amplifies their voice on the global stage but also serves as a deterrent against potential aggressors. In an increasingly interconnected world, the cooperative pursuit of self-sufficiency can empower small nations to stand firm against war mongering, reinforcing their sovereignty and ensuring their stability.

Grassroots movements and civil society

GRASSROOTS MOVEMENTS and civil society play a crucial role in shaping the response of small nations to the pressure exerted by larger powers. These movements often emerge from a deep-rooted desire for self-determination and the preservation of national identity in the face of external aggression. In many historical cases, grassroots organisations have mobilised communities to challenge foreign intervention and advocate for sovereignty, often using methods that highlight local culture, values, and traditions. By fostering a sense of unity and shared purpose, these movements can effectively counteract the disorienting effects of propaganda and the psychological warfare employed by aggressors.

The impact of foreign intervention on small nations is frequently exacerbated by the marginalisation of civil society. When external forces seek to impose their will, they often undermine local governance and erode public trust in institutions. In response, grassroots movements can emerge as vital platforms for civic engagement, empowering citizens to voice their concerns and resist external pressure. These movements not only address immediate issues related to sovereignty and autonomy but also work to rebuild social cohesion and resilience among the populace. Through awareness campaigns, peaceful protests, and community organising, they create a counter-narrative to the dominant discourse propagated by aggressors.

Historical case studies reveal that successful grassroots movements often draw upon shared experiences of oppression to galvanise support. For instance, in the face of colonial rule or military interventions, local leaders and activists have utilised storytelling and cultural expressions to articulate their struggles and aspirations. This approach not only fosters solidarity but also serves to educate the broader public, both domestically and internationally, about the injustices faced by their communities. By highlighting the human cost of war mongering, these movements can attract attention and sympathy, ultimately influencing public opinion and policy decisions in favor of the affected nations.

Nationalism also plays a significant role in the dynamics of grassroots movements within small nations. When faced with aggression, a revival of national pride can serve as a powerful motivator for collective action. Nationalist sentiments often encourage citizens to reclaim their history and identity, reinforcing their resistance against external pressures. Grassroots movements harness this energy, channeling it into organised efforts that seek to protect cultural heritage, promote political representation, and assert independence. As these movements gain traction, they can challenge the narratives pushed by larger powers, thereby fostering a more nuanced understanding of the complexities involved in these conflicts.

Strategies for small nations to resist bullying and aggression often hinge on the strength of their civil society and grassroots organizations. By building coalitions and alliances with other marginalised groups, small nations can amplify their voices and extend their reach. Engaging in strategic communication to counteract propaganda while promoting a narrative of resilience and unity is essential. Additionally, grassroots movements can seek international solidarity, leveraging global networks of activists and organisations to apply pressure on aggressors. Through these multifaceted approaches, small nations can empower their populations, reclaim their agency, and ultimately assert their right to self-determination in the face of overwhelming odds.

Utilising international law and organisations

INTERNATIONAL LAW AND organisations play a crucial role in providing small nations with frameworks for resistance against war mongering and aggression from larger powers. These legal instruments are designed to promote peace, security, and cooperation among states, offering smaller nations a means to assert their sovereignty and protect their interests. The United Nations, for instance, serves as a platform where small nations can voice their concerns, seek support, and potentially rally international opinion against aggressors. By engaging with these organisations, small nations can highlight their plight on a global stage, making it more difficult for larger nations to act unilaterally without facing international scrutiny.

The principles of international law, including the prohibition of the use of force and the right to self-determination, provide small nations with essential legal grounds to challenge acts of aggression. When larger states engage in military interventions or coercive diplomacy, small nations can invoke these principles to seek redress through international courts or bodies like the International Criminal Court. These legal avenues not only offer potential remedies but also serve to document and publicise instances of aggression, thereby reinforcing the narrative that such actions violate established norms and threaten global stability.

Moreover, regional organisations can also play a significant role in supporting small nations facing aggression. Organisations such as the African

Union, the Organization of American States, and the European Union can offer diplomatic support, economic assistance, and, in some cases, military aid to member states under threat. These regional bodies often have a better understanding of the specific geopolitical dynamics at play and can mobilise resources quickly to address crises. By collaborating within these frameworks, small nations can strengthen their collective defense and enhance their bargaining power against more formidable adversaries.

In addition to legal and organisational frameworks, small nations must also be strategic in their use of propaganda and communication to counteract narratives propagated by larger powers. The ability to shape public opinion is vital in garnering international support. By employing effective communication strategies, small nations can highlight their sovereignty, cultural identity, and the injustices they face, thereby framing their situation in a way that resonates with global audiences. This approach not only seeks to undermine the aggressor's legitimacy but also seeks to build alliances with other nations and civil society organizations that may be sympathetic to their cause.

Ultimately, the utilisation of international law and organisations, combined with strategic communication, provides small nations with a multifaceted approach to resisting war mongering and aggression. By actively engaging with the international community, small nations can bolster their sovereignty, challenge narratives that seek to delegitimise their actions, and foster a sense of solidarity among nations facing similar threats. In an increasingly interconnected world, the ability to leverage these tools effectively is essential for small nations striving to maintain their independence and protect their citizens from the consequences of external aggression.

Chapter 7: Conclusion

Lessons learned from historical case studies

The examination of historical case studies reveals critical lessons about the dynamics of war mongering against smaller nations. These instances often demonstrate a pattern of aggression fueled by a combination of economic interests, territorial ambitions, and a desire for geopolitical dominance. The stories of countries like Vietnam during the American War and Iraq in the early 2000s illustrate how larger powers exploit perceived vulnerabilities in smaller nations. The lessons drawn from these cases highlight the importance of recognising the motivations behind foreign interventions and the dire consequences they can have on a nation's sovereignty.

One prominent lesson is the role of propaganda in shaping public perception before and during conflicts. Historical case studies, such as the U.S. invasion of Iraq, showcase how misinformation and manipulation of the narrative can serve as precursors to military action. By portraying small nations as threats or aggressors, larger powers can justify their interventions. This tactic often leads to widespread support for military actions among the domestic population of the aggressor nation, while simultaneously undermining the target nation's legitimacy and sovereignty. Understanding these propaganda techniques is crucial for small nations seeking to protect themselves from potential aggression.

Case studies reveal that the aftermath of such interventions frequently leaves lasting scars on a nation's political and social fabric. For instance, in Libya, the initial intervention aimed at ousting a dictatorial regime spiraled into chaos, resulting in a fragmented state struggling with civil war and external influences. These experiences underscore the importance of resilience and the need for small nations to maintain their sovereignty amidst external pressures.

The maintenance of national identity and governance structures is vital in resisting the destabilizing effects of foreign intervention.

Another significant lesson involves the influence of nationalism in fostering unity within small nations facing aggression. Historical examples, such as the resistance movements in Eastern Europe during the Cold War, demonstrate how a strong sense of national identity can galvanize citizens against foreign threats. Nationalism can serve as a double-edged sword, however; while it can unite a populace, it can also lead to internal divisions if manipulated by external powers. Small nations must navigate this complex terrain carefully, fostering a sense of unity that prioritizes their sovereignty while remaining vigilant against the divisive tactics of larger powers.

Lastly, strategies for resistance must be developed based on historical precedents. Small nations can learn from the successes and failures of others in their struggle against bullying and aggression. Diplomatic engagement, forming strategic alliances, and leveraging international law can enhance their standing on the global stage. Moreover, investing in civic education to build a politically aware citizenry can empower the populace to recognize and resist external manipulation. By studying historical case studies of war mongering, small nations can devise informed strategies that bolster their resilience and autonomy in the face of potential threats.

The future of small nations in a globalised world

THE FUTURE OF SMALL nations in a globalized world is a topic that necessitates a nuanced understanding of the intricate dynamics at play. As globalization continues to reshape international relations, small nations find themselves grappling with both unprecedented opportunities and significant challenges. The interconnectedness fostered by globalization can enhance economic growth and cultural exchange, yet it simultaneously exposes these nations to the whims of larger powers that may seek to exploit their vulnerabilities. This duality creates a precarious position, where small nations must navigate the complexities of foreign influence and intervention while striving to maintain their sovereignty and identity.

One of the most pressing issues for small nations in this context is the increasing frequency and intensity of foreign intervention. Historical case studies illustrate how larger powers have often resorted to military force, economic sanctions, or covert operations to assert their dominance over smaller states. The lessons learned from these instances highlight the importance of international law and diplomatic engagement, which can serve as tools for small nations to resist external pressures. However, the effectiveness of these measures is frequently undermined by the geopolitical interests of more powerful countries, leading to a cycle of dependency and vulnerability that can be difficult to escape.

Propaganda techniques play a crucial role in the bullying of small nations, often serving as a precursor to more overt forms of aggression. The manipulation of public perception through disinformation campaigns can delegitimise the governance of small states and justify interventions under the guise of humanitarian or security concerns. An understanding of these techniques is essential for small nations, which must develop robust communication strategies to counter narratives that portray them as unstable or threatening. By fostering a strong national identity and promoting their own narratives, small nations can assert their agency in the face of external aggression.

The rise of nationalism within small nations can serve as both a shield and a sword in the struggle against external threats. A strong sense of national identity can unite citizens and foster resilience against foreign intervention, empowering them to advocate for their rights and sovereignty. However, nationalism can also lead to isolationism if taken to extremes, potentially undermining the very alliances and partnerships that small nations need to navigate the global landscape. Balancing these forces is critical for small nations, requiring a careful approach that values both national pride and international cooperation.

Ultimately, the strategies employed by small nations to resist bullying and aggression must be multifaceted and adaptable. Building coalitions with like-minded states, engaging in regional organisations, and leveraging international legal frameworks are vital components of a comprehensive strategy. Additionally, investing in education and public awareness can empower citizens to understand their role in promoting national resilience. As small nations continue to face the realities of a globalised world, their futures will depend on their ability to assert their sovereignty, engage critically with larger powers, and foster solidarity among themselves and their allies.

Call to action for awareness and support

THE CALL TO ACTION for awareness and support in the context of war mongering against small nations is imperative for fostering a more equitable and just global landscape. As we delve into the historical injustices faced by these vulnerable states, it becomes evident that a collective understanding and recognition of their plight is essential. The narratives of nations that have been subjected to aggression and manipulation must be amplified, as they highlight not only the consequences of power imbalances but also the resilience and agency of smaller nations in the face of adversity. By raising awareness, we can cultivate a sense of responsibility among the global community to stand against these injustices.

Public awareness is the first step in addressing the systemic issues that allow war mongering to thrive. Educational initiatives should be prioritized to inform citizens about the historical context of military interventions and the various propaganda techniques employed to justify such actions. These efforts can demystify the motivations behind foreign interventions and encourage critical thinking about the information presented by larger powers. Engaging the public through discussions, workshops, and multimedia campaigns can help to illuminate the experiences of small nations and foster empathy and solidarity among individuals who may not yet recognise their role in combating these injustices.

Support for small nations must extend beyond mere awareness; it requires tangible actions that affirm their sovereignty and right to self-determination. Advocacy groups and civil society organisations play a crucial role in this regard, as they can mobilise resources and leverage political pressure to address grievances faced by smaller nations. By collaborating with international bodies and human rights organisations, these groups can amplify the voices of those affected by war mongering, ensuring that their stories are not forgotten. Furthermore, promoting fair policies and practices in international relations can help create a more supportive environment for small nations, allowing them to thrive without the threat of external aggression.

Nationalism, when rooted in a genuine desire for self-determination, can be a powerful tool for small nations facing external pressures. Encouraging a healthy sense of national identity can foster unity among citizens, equipping them to resist bullying and aggression. However, it is crucial to differentiate between inclusive nationalism that celebrates diversity and exclusionary forms that may lead to xenophobia. Therefore, educational frameworks should emphasise the importance of solidarity not only within the nation but also with other vulnerable states. By building alliances and coalitions among small nations, they can collectively advocate for shared interests and resist the encroachments of larger powers.

Ultimately, the fight against war mongering and the support for small nations require a sustained effort from individuals, communities, and governments alike. By committing to ongoing education, advocacy, and the promotion of inclusive nationalism, we can create an environment that respects the sovereignty of all nations, irrespective of their size or power. It is essential for the global community to recognise the interconnectedness of our struggles and work collaboratively to dismantle the structures of oppression that allow war mongering to persist. The time for action is now, as each effort contributes to a more peaceful and just world for all nations.

Strategies for dissuasion

DISSUASION STRATEGIES are essential in promoting a culture of peace and preventing the escalation of conflicts. To effectively dissuade global warmongers, it is crucial to emphasise the moral, ethical, and practical reasons for pursuing peace over violence. Engaging in dialogues that focus on the consequences of war, including loss of life, destruction of communities, and long-term psychological trauma, can shift public sentiment against militaristic approaches. By highlighting stories of individuals and families affected by war, we can create a compelling narrative that underscores the urgent need to prioritise diplomacy and conflict resolution over aggression.

The psychological impact of war extends far beyond the battlefield. It affects not only combatants but also civilians, leading to widespread trauma, anxiety, and a breakdown in social cohesion. By raising awareness of these psychological consequences, we can foster empathy and understanding, which are vital components in dissuading warmongers. Educational initiatives that address the mental health ramifications of war can empower individuals to advocate for peace and challenge militaristic narratives. This approach can create a ripple effect, encouraging communities to prioritise mental well-being and stability over the allure of military solutions.

Economic considerations play a pivotal role in the discourse surrounding war and peace. The resources allocated to military spending could instead be invested in education, healthcare, and infrastructure, fostering sustainable development and stability. By presenting data and case studies that illustrate the economic burdens of militarism, including increased debt and reduced public services, dissuasion efforts can effectively appeal to the rational interests of governments and citizens alike. An economy that thrives on peace rather than conflict is not only more prosperous but also more resilient, making a compelling case for dissuading warmongers.

Historical case studies of successful peace movements provide valuable lessons in the strategies that can be employed to promote non-violence. By showcasing these successes, we can inspire current and future generations to adopt similar tactics in their quest for peace. The documentation and dissemination of these case studies are vital for building a robust narrative that counters militaristic ideologies and emphasises the effectiveness of peaceful dissuasion.

Environmental degradation is an often-overlooked consequence of armed conflict. Wars devastate ecosystems, displace populations, and lead to resource depletion, further complicating the quest for global peace. By linking the environmental costs of militarism to broader discussions on sustainability, we can create a more holistic dissuasion strategy that appeals to environmental advocates and peace activists alike. By promoting narratives that focus on the benefits of peace and the consequences of conflict, media outlets can influence public opinion, making dissuasion efforts more effective. as it provides a framework for accountability and conflict resolution, reinforcing the legitimacy of dissuasion strategies on a global scale.

Chapter 8:

The psychological impact of war

Trauma and mental health are critical factors that intertwine with the broader implications of war and conflict, affecting individuals and societies long after the cessation of hostilities. The psychological impact of trauma can manifest in various forms, including post-traumatic stress disorder (PTSD), anxiety, and depression. These conditions do not only affect veterans and combatants; civilians caught in the crossfire also experience significant psychological distress. As societies strive for peace, the mental health of affected populations must be prioritised to ensure that healing and recovery can take place, which is essential for sustainable peace efforts.

The psychological aftermath of war can impede progress towards global peace and stability. Individuals suffering from trauma may struggle to reintegrate into society, contributing to cycles of violence and unrest. The inability to process traumatic experiences can lead to increased aggression, mistrust among community members, and social fragmentation. Consequently, when mental health issues go unaddressed, they can undermine efforts to build consensus and foster cooperation in post-conflict environments. Addressing trauma is thus a vital step in dismantling the legacies of war and promoting a culture of peace.

The economic consequences of militarism extend beyond direct financial costs; they also encompass the long-term impacts on mental health. War consumes vast resources that could otherwise be channeled into mental health services, education, and community development. Countries engulfed in conflict often see their healthcare systems strained, limiting access to essential mental health care for those in need. As a result, the economic burden of untreated mental health issues can stifle recovery and growth, exacerbating societal instability and hindering efforts to secure lasting peace.

Historical case studies provide valuable insights into the relationship between trauma and successful peace movements. Many peace initiatives have been built on the foundation of acknowledging and addressing the psychological wounds inflicted by conflict. For instance, in post-apartheid South Africa, truth and reconciliation processes facilitated healing by allowing individuals to share their stories and confront their trauma in a supportive environment. Such approaches illustrate the importance of integrating mental health support into peacebuilding efforts, as they not only foster individual recovery but also promote collective healing and reconciliation.

The cycle of violence

THE CYCLE OF VIOLENCE is a pervasive phenomenon that undermines global peace and stability. It begins with the instigation of conflict, often fueled by political, economic, or ideological motivations. Once violence erupts, it creates a retaliatory atmosphere where affected parties feel compelled to respond in kind. This response can lead to a spiral of aggression that perpetuates itself, making resolution increasingly difficult. As violence begets violence, the initial grievances are often overshadowed by a growing sense of enmity and distrust, leading to a situation where dialogue and negotiation are eclipsed by hostility.

The psychological impact of war on individuals and communities plays a significant role in perpetuating this cycle. Survivors of violence often experience trauma, which can manifest as anxiety, depression, and post-traumatic stress disorder. These psychological scars affect not only the individuals directly involved but also their families and communities, creating a pervasive atmosphere of fear and anger. The longer the cycle of violence continues, the more entrenched these psychological effects become, making the prospect of reconciliation and peace increasingly elusive. As communities struggle to heal, the cycle can easily reignite with the slightest provocation.

Economically, militarism contributes to instability that further entrenches the cycle of violence. Resources that could be directed toward development, education, and social services are diverted to military spending and conflict management. This misallocation of resources exacerbates poverty and inequality, fostering resentment and desperation among marginalized populations. In turn, these conditions can lead to recruitment into armed groups or support for violent resistance movements, perpetuating the cycle. The economic consequences of warfare extend beyond the immediate conflict zone, affecting regional and global markets, leading to a broader destabilisation that can last for generations.

Historical case studies of successful peace movements provide valuable insights into breaking the cycle of violence. Movements led by figures such as Mahatma Gandhi and Martin Luther King Jr. demonstrate the power of nonviolent resistance and dialogue in overcoming entrenched conflict. These examples show that peace is not merely the absence of war but an active process that requires commitment, resilience, and a willingness to address underlying issues. By learning from these historical successes, contemporary movements can adopt strategies that promote understanding, reconciliation, and ultimately, a shift away from violence.

The influence of media on public perception of war and peace also plays a crucial role in the cycle of violence. Sensationalised reporting can exacerbate fear and division, while responsible journalism can foster understanding and empathy. Media outlets have the power to shape narratives around conflict, often contributing to the demonisation of perceived enemies. By promoting stories of peacebuilding and highlighting the human cost of war, the media can help cultivate a culture of peace that challenges the cycle of violence. Moreover, the importance of international law in preventing warfare cannot be overstated; it provides a framework for accountability and justice that can deter aggressors and promote peaceful resolutions to disputes.

Healing through peacebuilding

PEACEBUILDING SERVES as a crucial pathway to healing in societies marked by conflict and violence. It goes beyond the mere cessation of hostilities, focusing instead on the underlying issues that fuel discord. By fostering dialogue and understanding among conflicting parties, peacebuilding initiatives create environments where healing can begin. These efforts often involve community engagement, reconciliation processes, and creating spaces for shared narratives. When individuals and communities come together to address grievances and work towards mutual understanding, the psychological scars left by war can begin to mend, paving the way for a more peaceful society.

The psychological impact of war extends far beyond the battlefield; it affects entire communities and generations. Trauma experienced during conflicts can lead to long-lasting mental health issues, including anxiety, depression, and post-traumatic stress disorder. Peacebuilding efforts that prioritise mental health support can facilitate healing by providing individuals with the tools they need to process their experiences. Programs aimed at trauma recovery, such as counseling and community support groups, can help individuals share their stories and find solace in collective healing. By addressing the psychological wounds of war, societies can rebuild their social fabric and enhance resilience against future conflicts.

The economic consequences of militarism often exacerbate the challenges faced by post-conflict societies. Resources that could be allocated for development, education, and healthcare are frequently diverted to military expenditures, hindering economic growth and stability. Peacebuilding initiatives that focus on economic recovery can help redirect these resources towards rebuilding communities and fostering sustainable development. By investing in local economies, creating job opportunities, and supporting small businesses, peacebuilding can alleviate poverty and reduce the likelihood of future conflicts. Economic stability is intrinsically linked to peace, and therefore, prioritising economic recovery is essential for long-term healing.

Historical case studies illustrate the effectiveness of successful peace movements in promoting healing and reconciliation. Movements led by figures such as Mahatma Gandhi and Martin Luther King Jr. have shown that nonviolent resistance and dialogue can lead to significant social change. These examples underscore the importance of inclusive participation in peace processes, where diverse voices are heard and valued. By learning from these historical successes, contemporary peacebuilders can apply similar strategies to foster healing in post-conflict societies. The lessons learned from past movements can inspire new generations to pursue peaceful resolutions to their grievances.

Lastly, the role of international law in preventing warfare must be adhered to by all means although we have witnessed cases where these rules and laws are disregarded with no consequences. Legal frameworks establish norms and standards that discourage aggression and promote peaceful dispute resolution. By holding nations accountable for their actions and providing mechanisms for conflict resolution, international law serves as a vital tool in peacebuilding efforts. Strengthening international law can help create a global culture of peace, where respect for human rights and dignity becomes the foundation of international relations. That is why the idea of big brother protecting the wreck less habitual wrongdoer is unpalatable. When nations adhere to these legal standards, the likelihood of conflict diminishes, allowing societies to focus on healing and rebuilding rather than perpetual cycles of violence.

Chapter 9:

Economic Instability and War

The psychological impact of war extends beyond the battlefield, influencing economic conditions in profound ways. War-induced trauma can lead to decreased productivity as populations grapple with the psychological scars of conflict. This decline in human capital can stifle innovation and economic growth, making it difficult for societies to rebuild. Furthermore, the fear and uncertainty generated by armed conflicts can deter investment, both domestic and foreign, stunting economic recovery and perpetuating a cycle of poverty and instability.

Historical case studies illustrate how militarism can lead to economic disarray, often triggering a feedback loop that perpetuates violence. For instance, post-World War I Germany faced hyperinflation and economic collapse, conditions that fostered resentment and laid the groundwork for future conflicts. Similarly, the wars in the Middle East have devastated economies, leading to widespread unemployment and social unrest. These examples underscore the importance of addressing economic factors when seeking to resolve or prevent conflicts, as stable economies are foundational to maintaining peace.

Moreover, environmental degradation linked to armed conflicts further exacerbates economic instability. War often leads to the destruction of natural resources, such as forests and water supplies, which are vital for sustaining communities. This degradation can lead to food shortages, displacement, and increased competition for dwindling resources. As nations struggle with the fallout of environmental destruction, the likelihood of conflict increases, creating a cycle where economic instability and war feed into one another.

The influence of media on public perception plays a critical role in shaping attitudes toward war and peace. Sensationalised reporting can distort the realities of economic instability caused by conflict, often focusing on immediate violence rather than long-term consequences. This portrayal can lead to public apathy or support for militaristic policies, hindering efforts to prioritise peace. To counteract this, promoting awareness of the economic ramifications of war is essential in fostering a global understanding that prioritises peace over conflict. International law must also be upheld to hold aggressors accountable, thereby creating a framework that discourages militarism and promotes economic stability as a cornerstone of global peace efforts.

The financial implications of military spending are vast and multifaceted, impacting not just national budgets but also global economic stability. Countries allocate enormous resources to their armed forces, often at the expense of critical social programs such as education, healthcare, and infrastructure. This diversion of funds creates a ripple effect, leading to a decrease in the quality of life for citizens and an increase in social unrest. When governments prioritize military expenditures, the opportunity costs become apparent; essential services that could uplift communities and foster development are left underfunded, weakening the fabric of society.

Wealthier nations often invest heavily in advanced weaponry and defense systems, creating a power imbalance that can destabilise global relations. Developing countries may feel pressured to increase their military budgets in response, diverting funds from crucial development initiatives. This arms race can lead to inflated national debts, further straining economies and limiting the potential for growth and stability. Ultimately, such economic disparities contribute to a cycle of conflict, as nations may resort to militaristic strategies to assert their dominance or defend against perceived threats.

The constant emphasis on defense and warfare fosters a culture of fear and insecurity, which can lead to heightened anxiety among the population. This environment diminishes public trust in government and institutions, as citizens may feel that their leaders prioritise militarisation over their well-being. Furthermore, the normalisation of conflict in society can desensitise individuals to violence, eroding empathy and undermining efforts to promote peace. When the focus is skewed toward military might, the collective psyche of a nation can shift, making it increasingly difficult to advocate for peaceful resolutions to disputes.

Historical case studies of successful peace movements illustrate the potential benefits of reallocating military funds toward peaceful initiatives. For instance, the disarmament campaigns of the late 20th century not only demonstrated the power of grassroots activism but also highlighted how investments in diplomacy and social programs can yield positive outcomes. Countries that have embraced peace-centric policies often experience a reduction in violence and an increase in social cohesion. These examples serve as a potent reminder that prioritising peace over militarism can lead to sustainable prosperity and improved global relations.

The environmental degradation linked to armed conflicts is another critical consideration when evaluating military spending. Armed conflicts often result in significant ecological damage, from destroyed habitats to pollution caused by military operations. The resources spent on maintaining and expanding military capabilities could be redirected toward environmental conservation efforts, which are essential for global stability. By recognising the interconnectedness of military spending, environmental health, and peace, societies can work towards a more harmonious existence. The focus should shift from preparing for war to fostering conditions that promote lasting peace and sustainable development, reinforcing the idea that true security lies in cooperation rather than confrontation.

Redirecting resources to peaceful solutions requires a fundamental shift in how societies prioritize their investments. The global community faces pressing issues such as poverty, education, and healthcare, which can be addressed through peace-oriented policies rather than militaristic approaches. By reallocating funds traditionally earmarked for defense and military operations, nations can invest in conflict resolution initiatives, negotiation training, and community-building programs. This redirection not only fosters a more stable society but also enhances the overall quality of life for citizens, diminishing the allure of violent conflict.

The psychological impact of war extends far beyond the battlefield, influencing public perception and societal norms. The traumas of conflict can lead to entrenched cycles of violence, fear, and mistrust, which hinder peace efforts. Redirecting resources towards mental health services and community support can mitigate these effects. Programs focusing on trauma recovery and resilience-building can empower individuals and communities, creating a culture that prioritizes dialogue and understanding over aggression. In this way, the psychological scars of war can be addressed, fostering a healthier society less prone to conflict.

Economic considerations also play a crucial role in the discussion of redirecting resources. Militarism often diverts significant funds away from social programs, leading to stagnation in economic development. By investing in peace initiatives, countries can stimulate economic growth through job creation in sectors such as education, healthcare, and infrastructure. The economic benefits of a peaceful society include increased foreign investment, reduced healthcare costs related to conflict-related injuries, and enhanced productivity. Such investments not only bolster national economies but also contribute to global stability, as prosperous nations are less likely to engage in conflict.

Chapter 10:
Historical case studies of peace movements

Gandhi's philosophy of nonviolent resistance, or Satyagraha, serves as a powerful testament to the effectiveness of peaceful protest in the face of oppression. His methods were rooted in the belief that nonviolence is not just a tactic but a way of life that can bring about social change without the collateral damage often associated with armed conflict. By employing nonviolent strategies, Gandhi was able to mobilise millions of people in India against colonial rule, demonstrating that collective action grounded in peace can challenge even the most formidable powers. This approach not only helped India gain independence but also inspired numerous global movements advocating for civil rights and social justice.

The psychological impact of war on global peace efforts becomes starkly evident when contrasting it with Gandhi's ideology. War breeds trauma, fear, and division among communities, which in turn complicates the process of fostering dialogue and reconciliation. Gandhi believed that nonviolent resistance could heal societal wounds and build bridges across divides. By promoting understanding and respect among diverse groups, his approach directly counters the psychological scars left by war, emphasising the need for compassion and empathy in post-conflict societies. This healing aspect of nonviolence is crucial in preventing the cycle of violence that often perpetuates discord and instability.

Economically, the consequences of militarism can be detrimental to global stability, as resources are diverted from essential social services to fund armed conflicts. Gandhi's nonviolent resistance highlighted the potential for economic boycotts as a means of protest, which can effectively undermine oppressive regimes without resorting to violence. By advocating for self-sufficiency and local economies, he demonstrated how peaceful action could lead to economic empowerment and challenge the status quo. The lessons from Gandhi's strategies remind us that dissuading global warmongers requires not only a commitment to peace but also a recognition of the economic dimensions of conflict and resistance.

Historical case studies of successful peace movements reveal the profound impact of Gandhi's teachings beyond India. Figures such as Martin Luther King Jr. and Nelson Mandela drew inspiration from his principles, using nonviolent methods to challenge systemic injustice in their own contexts. These movements showcased how nonviolent resistance could effectively mobilise people and create significant political change, reinforcing the idea that peace can triumph over aggression. By studying these examples, contemporary movements can learn valuable lessons about organization, strategy, and the power of collective nonviolent action in the face of adversity.

War leads to significant ecological destruction, from deforestation to pollution, resulting in long-term consequences for communities and ecosystems. Gandhi's emphasis on the interconnectedness of all life aligns with the modern understanding of environmental stewardship as a form of resistance against militarism. By advocating for nonviolence, we can preserve not only human life but also the planet itself, fostering a sustainable future that prioritises peace over war.

In this context, the influence of media on public perception of war and peace becomes vital, as it shapes narratives that can either glorify violence or promote the values of nonviolent resistance, ultimately affecting policy and public opinion on global conflicts.

The civil rights movement

THE CIVIL RIGHTS MOVEMENT, a pivotal chapter in American history, was not only a struggle for racial equality but also a profound illustration of how collective action can challenge systemic injustice. Emerging in the mid-20th century, this movement galvanised diverse groups to advocate for civil rights, influencing social policies and reshaping public attitudes. It is essential to recognise how the principles and strategies employed during this era can inform contemporary efforts to dissuade global warmongers and promote lasting peace. The legacy of the Civil Rights Movement demonstrates that nonviolent resistance and grassroots mobilisation can yield significant societal change, a lesson that is particularly relevant in addressing the militaristic tendencies of nations today.

The psychological impact of war on societies can be profoundly understood through the lens of the Civil Rights Movement. Many activists faced severe threats, violence, and repression during their struggle for equality. This trauma not only affected the individuals directly involved but also reverberated throughout their communities, instilling a deep-seated fear and anxiety. The mental scars left by such conflicts underscore the importance of addressing the psychological consequences of military engagements

Economically, the Civil Rights Movement highlighted the intersection of social justice and financial equity. Discriminatory practices limited access to economic opportunities for marginalised communities, a reality that resonates with the economic consequences of militarism today. War diverts critical resources away from essential services like education and healthcare, exacerbating social inequalities. The lessons learned from the Civil Rights Movement show that investing in peace and social justice not only uplifts communities but also strengthens economies. By prioritising peace over militarisation, nations can cultivate environments that promote prosperity and reduce the likelihood of conflict.

wrought by war not only affects human lives but also devastates ecosystems, leading to long-term consequences for both the environment and public health. Recognising this connection is crucial for contemporary peace efforts, as advocates can frame the fight against militarism as an environmental imperative. By promoting peace, we also protect our planet, ensuring that future generations inherit a world where both social justice and ecological integrity are prioritised.

Recent years have seen a surge in global peace initiatives aimed at addressing the underlying causes of conflict and promoting a more peaceful world. These initiatives are often collaborative efforts involving governments, non-governmental organisations, and grassroots movements. One prominent example is the United Nations' Sustainable Development Goals (SDGs), which aim to eradicate poverty, promote education, and ensure justice, all of which are foundational to long-term peace.

Another significant initiative is the role of citizen diplomacy, where ordinary people engage in dialogue and cooperation across borders. Programs such as Sister Cities and Youth Exchange initiatives foster relationships between communities in different countries, promoting understanding and collaboration. These grassroots efforts can counteract the narratives of fear and division often propagated by media outlets and political rhetoric. By building personal connections, these initiatives help to humanise individuals from different backgrounds, making it more difficult for warmongers to justify conflict over cooperation.

International law also plays a crucial role in recent peace initiatives. Treaties and agreements, such as the Paris Agreement on climate change, demonstrate how global cooperation can address issues that transcend national borders. By framing environmental degradation as a collective responsibility, these agreements not only aim to protect the planet but also serve as platforms for diplomacy. When nations commit to working together on shared challenges, they create opportunities for dialogue and collaboration, reducing the likelihood of militaristic responses to perceived threats.

The influence of media cannot be understated in shaping public perception of war and peace. Recent initiatives have sought to promote responsible journalism that emphasises peaceful conflict resolution and highlights stories of successful peace efforts. Media campaigns that focus on the human cost of war and the benefits of peace can shift public opinion, creating a demand for policies that prioritise diplomacy over militarism. By showcasing positive narratives and the effectiveness of peace initiatives, media can play a vital role in fostering a culture that values dialogue and understanding.

Lastly, historical case studies of successful peace movements provide valuable insights and inspiration for current initiatives. Movements such as the anti-apartheid struggle in South Africa and the civil rights movement in the United States illustrate the power of nonviolent resistance and the importance of collective action. These examples highlight how sustained efforts by ordinary people can lead to significant political and social change.

Environmental degradation and armed conflicts

THE DESTRUCTION OF ecosystems is one of the most profound and often overlooked consequences of armed conflict. Wars disrupt not only human lives but also the delicate balance of nature. Armed conflicts lead to deforestation, soil degradation, and the pollution of air and water resources. The immediate impacts of military actions, such as bombings and the movement of troops, can devastate habitats and biodiversity. These changes are not merely temporary; they can have long-lasting effects that destabilise the environment and diminish the resources needed for human survival.

In many regions, the aftermath of war sees a surge in illegal logging, mining, and poaching as desperate populations seek to rebuild their livelihoods. The collapse of governance during conflicts often leads to unregulated exploitation of natural resources. For example, in war-torn countries, the absence of law enforcement allows for the rampant destruction of forests, which not only contributes to climate change but also threatens the lives of numerous species. The resultant loss of biodiversity can alter ecosystems irreversibly, leading to a decline in ecosystem services that are vital for human health and well-being, such as clean water and fertile soil.

The relationship between militarism and environmental degradation extends beyond the immediate battlefield. Military operations often require vast amounts of resources, leading to unsustainable practices that impact ecosystems far from the conflict zones. The production and testing of weapons, for instance, can result in toxic waste and pollution that infiltrate local environments, affecting both human and wildlife populations. This phenomenon can create a cycle of degradation that further exacerbates the challenges of recovery and reconstruction in post-conflict societies.

Psychologically, the destruction of ecosystems influences not only the environment but also the mental health of communities. Individuals exposed to the ravages of war and the subsequent loss of their surroundings may experience heightened levels of stress, anxiety, and depression. The connection between people and their environment is vital for cultural identity and community cohesion. When ecosystems are destroyed, the psychological impact can hinder peace efforts, as communities struggle to rebuild their lives amidst the ruins of their natural heritage.

Addressing the destruction of ecosystems caused by warfare requires a concerted effort to promote peace and dissuade global warmongers. International law plays a crucial role in this regard, as it establishes frameworks for environmental protection in times of conflict. By prioritizing peace over war, societies can work toward sustainable development that respects both human and ecological well-being. Emphasizing the importance of environmental stewardship in peace negotiations could lead to more resilient communities and healthier ecosystems, ultimately fostering a more stable and peaceful world for future generations.

The intersection of resource scarcity and climate change has become increasingly relevant in contemporary discussions about global conflict. As natural resources such as water, arable land, and fossil fuels become more limited due to environmental degradation, competition for these resources intensifies. This competition can lead to violent confrontations, often referred to as "resource wars." These conflicts not only exacerbate existing tensions but also contribute to further environmental degradation, creating a vicious cycle that undermines global peace efforts. Understanding this dynamic is essential for dissuading global warmongers and promoting a more harmonious world.

Climate change plays a pivotal role in exacerbating resource scarcity. Rising temperatures, shifting precipitation patterns, and extreme weather events can drastically affect agricultural productivity and water availability. As communities struggle to adapt to these changes, the potential for conflict increases. For instance, in regions where water resources are shared, such as transboundary river basins, the pressure to secure access can lead to disputes and, ultimately, armed conflict. Highlighting these connections helps illustrate the urgent need for international cooperation and conflict resolution to address the underlying causes of resource wars.

Armed conflicts often result in significant trauma for affected populations, leading to long-lasting effects on mental health and community cohesion. The fear and anxiety generated by resource wars can foster a culture of militarism, where societies become more accepting of violence as a means of resolving disputes. This mindset poses a significant barrier to achieving lasting peace and stability, emphasising the importance of addressing the root causes of conflict, including those driven by resource scarcity and climate change.

DISSUADING WAR MONGERS

Economically, the consequences of militarism can further destabilise regions already vulnerable to the impacts of climate change. Resources that could be allocated towards sustainable development and climate adaptation are often diverted to military expenditure. This not only stifles economic growth but also hampers efforts to build resilience against climate change. The prioritisation of military solutions over diplomatic ones can exacerbate resource-related conflicts, making it essential to advocate for peaceful alternatives that prioritize human security and environmental sustainability.

To counter these trends, international law plays a crucial role in preventing warfare and promoting peace. Legal frameworks that regulate resource management, protect the environment, and facilitate dispute resolution can help mitigate the risk of resource wars. Strengthening international cooperation and commitment to these laws is vital in creating a global environment where dialogue and collaboration take precedence over conflict. By fostering a culture of peace and respect for human rights, the international community can better address the challenges posed by climate change and resource scarcity, ultimately dissuading the global warmongers and working towards a more peaceful future.

Sustainable peace practices are essential for fostering an environment where conflicts can be resolved without resorting to violence. These practices encompass a range of strategies that prioritise dialogue, understanding, and cooperation over militaristic approaches. By promoting sustainable peace, societies can create frameworks that not only prevent war but also address the underlying issues that contribute to conflict. This involves engaging diverse stakeholders, including local communities, governments, and international organisations, to collaboratively identify and implement solutions that honor human rights and promote social justice.

One of the core components of sustainable peace practices is the emphasis on dialogue and mediation. Conflict resolution through peaceful means can significantly reduce the psychological impact of war on affected populations. By facilitating open communication and understanding, communities can work towards reconciling differences and building trust. This approach not only mitigates the immediate tensions that can lead to violence but also fosters a culture of peace that can prevent future conflicts. Programs that encourage community dialogue, promote empathy, and offer conflict resolution training are vital in this regard, as they empower individuals to handle disputes constructively.

Historical case studies of successful peace movements offer valuable lessons for implementing sustainable peace practices. Various movements around the world have demonstrated that organised, non-violent resistance can lead to significant political and social change. These movements often harness collective action to challenge unjust systems and promote peaceful alternatives. By studying these examples, contemporary activists and policymakers can glean insights into effective strategies for mobilising communities, creating alliances, and advocating for systemic change. A focus on grassroots organising and the empowerment of marginalised voices is crucial in replicating these successes in today's context.

Chapter 11:
Media's role in war and peace

The Power of Narrative shapes our understanding of world events, particularly in the context of war and peace. In a global landscape often dominated by militaristic rhetoric, the stories we tell about conflict and resolution profoundly influence public perception and policy. Narratives have the capacity to either glorify violence or promote understanding and reconciliation. By focusing on the power of narrative, we can challenge the prevailing discourse that often legitimises war, urging a shift toward narratives that prioritise peace and cooperation.

Narratives that highlight the human cost of conflict resonate deeply with individuals and communities, fostering empathy and understanding. When stories of loss, suffering, and resilience are shared, they can break down barriers of indifference and promote a collective desire for peace. By amplifying these narratives, we can create a powerful counter-narrative to the glorification of war, demonstrating that peace is not only possible but also preferable for the psychological well-being of societies.

Economically, the consequences of militarism are often overshadowed by the allure of national security rhetoric. Narratives that frame military spending as a necessary evil can obscure the reality of its detrimental effects on global stability. By recalibrating the narrative to emphasize the economic benefits of peace—such as increased trade, investment in social infrastructure, and the potential for sustainable development—we can encourage public support for dissuading warmongers. Highlighting historical case studies that showcase economic prosperity following peace agreements can further reinforce this narrative.

Promoting peace through journalism

PROMOTING PEACE THROUGH journalism is a vital aspect of fostering a global environment where dialogue and understanding can thrive over conflict. Journalists have the unique ability to shape narratives, influence public opinion, and highlight the often-overlooked consequences of war. By focusing on stories that emphasize peace, cooperation, and the shared humanity of people across borders, journalism can serve as a powerful tool in dissuading global warmongers and advocating for peaceful resolutions to conflicts. It is essential for media outlets to prioritise reporting on successful peace initiatives and the positive outcomes of diplomacy, thereby countering the prevalent narratives that glorify militarism and warfare.

Journalism can play a crucial role in addressing these psychological scars by providing a platform for the voices of those who have experienced the horrors of conflict. By sharing personal stories of resilience and healing, the media can encourage empathy and understanding among audiences, fostering a culture that values peace over violence. Furthermore, highlighting the mental health challenges faced by veterans, refugees, and civilians can galvanise public support for mental health resources and policies aimed at healing the wounds of war.

Historical case studies of successful peace movements provide valuable lessons for current and future efforts to promote peace. Journalists can play a pivotal role in documenting these movements, analysing their strategies, and disseminating their stories to inspire others. By showcasing the power of grassroots activism and nonviolent resistance, media narratives can motivate individuals and communities to advocate for change. Additionally, highlighting the successes of peace movements reinforces the idea that achieving lasting peace is possible and that collective action can lead to tangible results.

Journalists must strive to present balanced and nuanced accounts of conflicts, avoiding sensationalism that can desensitise audiences to the human cost of war. By reporting on the importance of international law in preventing warfare and the role it plays in holding aggressors accountable, the media can help cultivate a culture of respect for human rights and diplomatic solutions. Ultimately, promoting peace through journalism requires a commitment to ethical reporting and a dedication to amplifying the voices that advocate for a world free from the ravages of war.

Chapter 12:
International law and warfare prevention

International treaties play a crucial role in maintaining global peace and security by establishing frameworks for cooperation, conflict resolution, and the promotion of human rights among nations. These legally binding agreements serve as tools for diplomacy, enabling countries to negotiate their interests and resolve disputes without resorting to armed conflict. By fostering dialogue and mutual understanding, international treaties help create an environment conducive to peace, where nations can address their grievances through peaceful means rather than military action. The significance of these treaties is underscored by their ability to codify norms and standards that discourage aggressive behavior and promote cooperation among states.

One of the most important aspects of international treaties is their role in dissuading global warmongers. Treaties like the United Nations Charter and various arms control agreements set clear expectations for state behavior, emphasising the importance of peaceful resolution of disputes. When countries commit to these agreements, they signal a collective willingness to prioritise dialogue over warfare. Additionally, the presence of such treaties can act as a deterrent against potential aggressors, as violating international law could lead to diplomatic isolation, sanctions, or other forms of international accountability. This framework creates a more stable global environment, reducing the likelihood of conflict.

International treaties that promote peace and cooperation can help mitigate the trauma and societal divisions caused by armed conflict. By fostering a culture of peace, these treaties encourage nations to invest in social programs, economic development, and education, rather than militarisation. This shift in focus can lead to healthier societies that are less prone to violence, as communities that experience the benefits of peace are more likely to advocate for its continuation. The psychological healing facilitated by international agreements can have long-lasting effects on communities that have experienced conflict, reinforcing the importance of such treaties in post-war recovery.

Economically, treaties that prioritise peace and disarmament can contribute significantly to global stability.

The historical success of various peace movements showcases the power of international treaties in achieving lasting peace. Case studies, such as the Treaty of Versailles and the various peace accords that followed World War II, illustrate how diplomatic agreements have played pivotal roles in resolving conflicts and preventing future wars. Additionally, these treaties often incorporate mechanisms for enforcement and dispute resolution, ensuring that nations adhere to their commitments. The continued evolution of international law reflects the global community's understanding of the necessity of such frameworks in promoting peace and preventing warfare. As the world faces new challenges, the role of international treaties remains vital in dissuading global warmongers and fostering a culture of peace.

Accountability for war crimes

THE CONCEPT OF ACCOUNTABILITY for war crimes serves as a crucial pillar in the pursuit of global peace. War crimes, which encompass grave violations of human rights and international law during armed conflicts, must not go unpunished if the international community is to foster a culture of respect for human dignity and peace. Holding individuals and nations accountable for their actions during war is essential in deterring future atrocities and ensuring that the consequences of such actions are clearly understood. This accountability extends to both state actors and non-state entities, emphasising that no one is above the law, thus reinforcing the principle that peace must be upheld through justice.

International law plays a significant role in establishing norms and standards for accountability. Institutions such as the International Criminal Court (ICC) have been created to prosecute individuals accused of war crimes, crimes against humanity, and genocide. These legal frameworks not only provide a mechanism for justice but also signal to the global community that violations will have repercussions. The existence of such institutions is imperative for preventing the normalisation of violence and abuse, as they hold perpetrators accountable and provide a sense of justice for victims.

In instances where traditional legal systems fail, international mechanisms fill the gaps, demonstrating the importance of a robust legal framework in promoting peace.

The psychological impact of war crimes extends beyond immediate victims; it resonates throughout societies and generations. Survivors of war crimes often suffer from long-term trauma, which can impede community healing and reconciliation efforts. This intergenerational trauma can foster an environment of distrust and resentment, undermining attempts to build stable, peaceful societies. By ensuring accountability for war crimes, the international community can help facilitate healing processes, thereby promoting psychological recovery and fostering a collective commitment to peace and coexistence. The acknowledgment of suffering through accountability can also empower victims and communities to engage in peace-building efforts.

The economic consequences of militarism are intertwined with the need for accountability in wartime actions. War crimes often lead to significant destruction of infrastructure, loss of livelihoods, and disruption of economies. When accountability is pursued, it can contribute to economic recovery by restoring order and instilling confidence in governance. Furthermore, victims of war crimes may receive reparations, which may aid in rebuilding their lives and communities. Dissuading global warmongers from engaging in conflict through the establishment of accountability mechanisms not only addresses moral and ethical concerns but also contributes to long-term economic stability and prosperity.

Historical case studies of successful peace movements highlight the effectiveness of accountability in fostering peace. Instances such as post-apartheid South Africa, where the Truth and Reconciliation Commission played a pivotal role in addressing past atrocities, demonstrate how accountability can lead to societal healing and progress. These examples illustrate that accountability for war crimes is not merely a punitive measure but a necessary step toward creating an environment conducive to lasting peace. By learning from these successes, the global community can advocate for stronger mechanisms to hold perpetrators accountable, thereby promoting the principles of justice and peace that are essential for a stable and harmonious world.

Strengthening global governance for peace requires a concerted effort to create frameworks that prioritise diplomacy over conflict.

One of the primary objectives should be to enhance international institutions and treaties that promote peaceful resolution of disputes. This can include reforming the United Nations to ensure that it has the necessary authority to intervene in conflicts and enforce peace agreements effectively. By strengthening these global governance structures, nations can work collaboratively to address issues that could lead to war, thereby fostering a more peaceful global environment.

The psychological impact of war on individuals and societies underscores the necessity for a robust global governance system. War inflicts deep psychological scars, leading to long-term trauma that can perpetuate cycles of violence and instability. Strengthening governance structures can facilitate mental health support and rehabilitation for affected populations, promoting healing and reconciliation. Through international cooperation and commitment to peace, countries can address the mental health crises that often follow armed conflicts, thereby diminishing the likelihood of future wars.

Economic consequences of militarism present another compelling reason for strengthening global governance. Military spending diverts essential resources that could otherwise be used for social welfare, education, and healthcare. By fostering international economic cooperation and development initiatives, nations can address the root causes of conflict, such as poverty and inequality. A governance framework that emphasises economic stability over militarisation can lead to a more secure world, reducing the incentives for war and promoting sustainable development.

Historical case studies of successful peace movements offer valuable insights into the effectiveness of global governance in fostering peace. Movements that have successfully advocated for nonviolent solutions demonstrate the power of collective action in influencing policy change. By learning from these examples, global governance can incorporate strategies that empower civil society and grassroots movements, ensuring that peace becomes a shared goal rather than an abstract ideal. Encouraging collaborative initiatives can help bridge divides and foster understanding among nations.

Strengthening global governance involves reinforcing legal frameworks that hold nations accountable for acts of aggression. By establishing clear consequences for violations of international law, the international community can deter potential aggressors and promote a culture of accountability. Furthermore, enhancing the role of the International Criminal Court and other legal bodies can provide mechanisms for conflict resolution that prioritise justice and peace over military intervention. In this way, a robust system of global governance can help ensure that the principles of peace are upheld, ultimately leading to a more harmonious world.

Chapter 13: The evolution of warfare

The historical context of military innovations reveals a consistent pattern of adaptation and evolution driven by technological advancements and the changing nature of warfare. From the introduction of gunpowder in the Middle Ages to the development of the atomic bomb in the 20th century, military forces have continually sought to leverage new technologies to gain strategic advantages. Each significant leap in military capability has been accompanied by shifts in tactics, strategy, and even the structure of armed forces. Understanding this trajectory is essential for grasping how contemporary innovations, such as skiving data crafts and autonomous drone warfare, might reshape the battlefield of the future.

The industrial revolution marked a turning point in military innovation, introducing mechanisation and mass production to warfare. The use of railroads for troop movement and telegraph systems for communication fundamentally altered operational logistics. World War I saw the first widespread use of tanks and aircraft, which transformed ground and aerial combat dynamics. These advancements not only increased the scale and lethality of warfare but also underscored the importance of technological supremacy in military strategy. The lessons learned during this era continue to influence modern militaries as they integrate advanced robotics and AI-driven intelligence analysis into their operational frameworks.

The Cold War era further accelerated military innovations, with both superpowers investing heavily in research and development to maintain a competitive edge. The space race led to breakthroughs in satellite technology, which have become indispensable for modern reconnaissance and communication. The emergence of cyber warfare as a new theater of conflict has its roots in this period as well, with nations recognising the potential of electronic systems for both offense and defense. As contemporary conflicts increasingly involve cyber capabilities, it is crucial to understand the historical precedents that paved the way for current cybersecurity strategies and practices.

In recent decades, the pace of military innovation has only intensified, driven by advancements in artificial intelligence, quantum computing, and sustainable energy solutions. The development of autonomous systems, such as drones, has revolutionised reconnaissance and strike capabilities, allowing for operations with reduced risk to human life. Similarly, augmented reality is transforming tactical training, providing soldiers with immersive simulations that enhance readiness and adaptability. These innovations highlight a shift towards more integrated and technologically sophisticated military operations, emphasising the need for robust cybersecurity measures to protect increasingly complex systems.

As we look to the future, the integration of biometric security and identification, space-based defense systems, and wearable technology for soldiers represents the culmination of a historical journey marked by innovation and adaptation. Military forces are not only investing in new technologies but are also rethinking their operational strategies to align with the capabilities these technologies provide. The historical context of military innovations serves as a reminder that while the tools of warfare may change, the underlying principles of strategy, adaptability, and the quest for superiority remain constant. Understanding this evolution is vital for anticipating the future of military operations in an era defined by rapid technological change.

The role of technology in shaping conflicts

THE ROLE OF TECHNOLOGY in shaping conflicts has evolved dramatically over the past few decades, fundamentally altering the landscape of modern warfare. As nations invest heavily in advanced technologies, the methods and strategies employed in conflicts are being redefined. From autonomous drone warfare to cyber capabilities, the integration of sophisticated tools has enabled military forces to operate in ways that were once deemed impossible. This transformation enhances combat effectiveness and also introduces new ethical and strategic considerations that must be addressed.

Autonomous drones have emerged as a pivotal element in contemporary military operations. These unmanned aerial vehicles are capable of conducting surveillance and precision strikes without direct human intervention. The ability to deploy drones for intelligence, reconnaissance, and combat missions allows for greater operational flexibility and reduced risk to personnel. However, the increasing reliance on such technology raises questions about accountability and the potential for miscalculations in high-stakes environments. As autonomous systems become more prevalent, the importance of establishing clear rules of engagement and oversight measures is paramount to prevent unintended escalations.

In parallel with drone technology, cyber warfare has become a critical battleground in modern conflicts. Nations are increasingly targeting each other's critical infrastructure, financial systems, and communication networks through cyberattacks. This shift from traditional kinetic warfare to cyber operations necessitates a robust cybersecurity framework to protect vital assets and maintain operational integrity. As military organisations enhance their cyber capabilities, the need for trained personnel and advanced defensive technologies becomes essential. The interconnectedness of global networks means that a breach can have far-reaching implications, making cybersecurity a top priority for national defense strategies.

Advanced robotics in combat further exemplifies how technology is reshaping military engagements. Robots can perform various tasks in hazardous environments, from bomb disposal to logistics support. Their deployment not only enhances safety for soldiers but also improves efficiency in operations. However, the integration of robotics into warfare also prompts concerns regarding the potential for autonomous systems to make life-and-death decisions without human oversight. Striking a balance between leveraging these technologies and maintaining ethical standards in combat will be crucial as militaries continue to innovate.

Emerging technologies, such as augmented reality for tactical training and AI-driven intelligence analysis, are revolutionising how soldiers prepare for and engage in conflict. Augmented reality can simulate real-world scenarios, providing soldiers with immersive training experiences that improve decision-making skills under pressure. Meanwhile, AI-driven analysis of vast amounts of data enables military leaders to gain insights and make strategic decisions more effectively. As these technologies advance, they will likely lead to a new era of warfare characterised by precision, efficiency, and potentially, a redefinition of what it means to engage in conflict. The integration of such innovations into military operations not only enhances capabilities but also requires ongoing assessment of their implications for future battles.

The emergence of data-driven warfare

THE EMERGENCE OF DATA-driven warfare marks a significant shift in the landscape of military operations, fundamentally altering how conflicts are conceived and executed. This new paradigm leverages vast amounts of information derived from various sources, including satellite imagery, social media analytics, and real-time battlefield intelligence. As militaries worldwide adopt data-centric approaches, the integration of advanced technologies enables them to make faster and more informed decisions. The ability to analyse and utilise data effectively has become a critical determinant of success in modern combat scenarios.

Autonomous drone warfare exemplifies the application of data-driven strategies in military operations. Drones equipped with sophisticated sensors and artificial intelligence algorithms can gather intelligence, conduct surveillance, and even engage targets with minimal human intervention. These advancements not only enhance operational efficiency but also reduce the risk to personnel. However, the reliance on autonomous systems raises ethical and strategic questions, particularly regarding accountability in decision-making processes and the implications of machine-driven warfare.

Cyber warfare has become an integral component of data-driven military strategies, with nations increasingly recognising the importance of securing their digital infrastructure. Cyber-attacks can disrupt communications, manipulate information, and compromise critical systems, potentially leading to significant operational setbacks. In response, militaries are investing heavily in cybersecurity measures to protect sensitive data and ensure the integrity of their operations. This focus on cyber defense underscores the necessity of a comprehensive strategy that encompasses both offensive and defensive capabilities in the digital realm.

Advanced robotics and wearable technology are also transforming the battlefield experience for soldiers. Robots can be deployed for dangerous missions such as bomb disposal or reconnaissance, minimising human exposure to perilous situations. Meanwhile, wearable devices equipped with biometric sensors provide soldiers with real-time health monitoring and situational awareness, enabling them to perform at optimal levels. These innovations not only enhance individual soldier capabilities but also contribute to the collective effectiveness of military units in dynamic environments.

As data-driven warfare continues to evolve, emerging technologies such as quantum computing and space-based defense systems are poised to redefine military strategy further. Quantum computing offers unprecedented processing power, enabling rapid analysis of complex datasets and simulations that can inform tactical decisions. Additionally, space-based systems enhance surveillance and communication capabilities, providing a strategic advantage in both offensive and defensive operations. Collectively, these advancements underscore the critical role of data and technology in shaping the future of warfare, where success will increasingly depend on the ability to harness and interpret information in real-time.

Chapter 14: Skiving data crafts

Definition and functionality

The term "skiving data crafts" refers to advanced technological systems designed to manipulate and utilize data in innovative ways for military purposes. These crafts are not limited to traditional aircraft or vehicles; they encompass a broad range of platforms, including autonomous drones, robotic units, and ground-based systems that gather, analyze, and disseminate information in real-time. At their core, skiving data crafts leverage the power of data to enhance situational awareness, optimize decision-making processes, and ultimately improve operational effectiveness on the battlefield. This capability is particularly critical in modern warfare, where information dominance can determine the outcome of engagements.

The functionality of skiving data crafts is rooted in their ability to integrate various technologies, including artificial intelligence, machine learning, and advanced sensors. These systems can autonomously gather intelligence from multiple sources, process vast amounts of data, and provide actionable insights to commanders and personnel. For instance, an autonomous drone equipped with high-resolution imaging and real-time data processing can survey a battlefield, detect enemy positions, and relay that information to troops on the ground, significantly enhancing their tactical advantage. This integration allows for a more agile and responsive approach to warfare, where decisions can be made swiftly based on the most current intelligence.

Moreover, skiving data crafts often operate in conjunction with other emerging technologies, such as augmented reality and wearable technology. Soldiers equipped with augmented reality systems can visualise data overlays in their field of vision, providing them with critical information about their environment without needing to divert their attention. Wearable technology can monitor a soldier's physiological status and integrate this data into the broader operational framework, ensuring that commanders are aware of their troops' readiness and health. This interconnectedness not only improves individual performance but also enhances team cohesion and operational synergy.

In the context of cybersecurity, skiving data crafts must also prioritise the protection of sensitive information. As military operations increasingly rely on interconnected systems, the risk of cyber threats becomes a significant concern. Skiving data crafts incorporate advanced cybersecurity measures to safeguard data integrity, ensuring that the information used for decision-making is accurate and secure from adversaries. By employing techniques such as biometric security and encryption, these systems can protect against unauthorised access and manipulation, thereby maintaining trust in the data that informs military strategy.

Finally, the functionality of skiving data crafts extends beyond traditional combat scenarios. They play a vital role in sustainable energy solutions for military operations, utilising energy-efficient technologies and renewable sources to reduce logistical footprints. This not only enhances operational sustainability but also aligns with global efforts to minimise environmental impact. As military forces evolve to meet the challenges of future warfare, skiving data crafts will be instrumental in shaping a more effective, secure, and sustainable approach to defense, ensuring that they remain at the forefront of innovation in military strategy.

Applications in modern warfare

IN MODERN WARFARE, the integration of advanced technology has transformed the battlefield into a complex environment where traditional tactics meet cutting-edge innovations. One of the most significant advancements is the use of skiving data crafts, which are designed to gather and analyse vast amounts of information in real-time. These crafts utilise sophisticated algorithms to filter through data, providing military strategists with crucial insights that enhance decision-making processes. By harnessing the power of big data, military forces can anticipate enemy movements, optimise resource allocation, and improve operational efficiency, ultimately gaining a strategic advantage over adversaries.

Autonomous drone warfare represents another pivotal shift in military operations. Unmanned aerial vehicles (UAVs) equipped with artificial intelligence can conduct surveillance, reconnaissance, and even combat missions without the direct involvement of human operators. This technology reduces the risk to personnel and allows for precise strikes on high-value targets. Moreover, the ability of drones to operate in swarm formations presents a new tactical approach, enabling coordinated attacks that can overwhelm enemy defenses. The implications of such capabilities extend beyond immediate combat, as they also raise ethical considerations and necessitate discussions on rules of engagement in an increasingly automated warfare landscape.

Cyber warfare has emerged as a critical front in modern military engagements, where the stakes are as high as those in traditional combat. Military forces are investing heavily in cybersecurity measures to protect sensitive information and infrastructure from malicious attacks. Advanced tactics such as hacking, denial-of-service attacks, and information warfare are now integral components of military strategy. The ability to disrupt an enemy's communication networks or critical systems can tilt the balance of power in favour of the attacker. As nations increasingly rely on digital systems, the importance of robust cybersecurity protocols cannot be overstated, making it an essential aspect of future military operations.

Advanced robotics in combat further revolutionizes the way armed forces engage with threats. Robotic systems are being developed for various roles, from bomb disposal units to front-line combat support. These machines can operate in environments that are too dangerous for human soldiers, minimising casualties and enhancing mission success rates. The development of humanoid robots capable of performing complex tasks on the battlefield signifies a move toward a hybrid force structure, where humans and machines collaborate. This synergy not only improves operational capabilities but also raises questions about the future of soldier roles and the ethical implications of robotic warfare.

The integration of augmented reality (AR) for tactical training represents a significant evolution in how soldiers prepare for combat. AR technology can simulate real-world scenarios, allowing troops to practice their skills in a controlled, immersive environment. This approach enhances learning experiences and helps soldiers develop critical decision-making abilities under pressure. Additionally, AI-driven intelligence analysis tools are streamlining the processing of battlefield data, enabling rapid assessment and response to emerging threats. As military forces continue to embrace innovations like wearable technology, quantum computing, and space-based defense systems, it is clear that the future of warfare will be shaped by a combination of advanced technologies designed to enhance effectiveness, security, and sustainability in military operations.

Ethical considerations

ETHICAL CONSIDERATIONS in the context of future warfare are increasingly vital as military operations evolve with advancements in technology. The integration of skiving data crafts, autonomous drone warfare, and AI-driven intelligence analysis raises profound moral questions about the role of human judgment in combat. One critical concern is the potential for dehumanisation in warfare, where decisions are made by algorithms rather than individuals. This shift can lead to a detachment from the moral implications of military actions, as automated systems may prioritise mission success over the preservation of human life.

The use of advanced robotics in combat introduces additional ethical dilemmas. While these technologies can enhance operational efficiency and reduce risks to human soldiers, they also raise questions about accountability. In scenarios where robots are involved in lethal actions, determining responsibility for mistakes or unintended consequences becomes complex. The challenge lies in establishing clear guidelines that define the limits of robotic engagement and ensure that human oversight remains a fundamental aspect of military operations.

Cyber warfare and cybersecurity present unique ethical challenges as well. The potential for collateral damage in cyberspace, where civilian infrastructure can be inadvertently compromised, necessitates a reevaluation of traditional wartime ethics. The principles of distinction and proportionality, which guide conventional warfare, must be adapted to account for the realities of digital conflict. This requires the military to develop robust ethical frameworks that prioritise the protection of non-combatants while still addressing the strategic imperatives of cyber operations.

As soldiers become increasingly connected through devices that monitor their health and performance, the potential for misuse of personal data grows. It is essential to establish standards that protect soldiers' privacy while ensuring that the benefits of these technologies can be fully realised. The balance between operational efficiency and individual rights must be carefully managed to maintain trust within the ranks.

Lastly, the potential use of quantum computing in military strategy introduces a new layer of ethical consideration. The ability to process vast amounts of data at unprecedented speeds could lead to significant advantages in warfare. However, this power must be wielded responsibly to prevent escalation and maintain global stability. As nations race to harness quantum technology, international agreements and ethical guidelines will be crucial in ensuring that its application in military contexts does not exacerbate tensions or lead to catastrophic consequences. Addressing these ethical considerations is essential for shaping a future of warfare that is not only effective but also aligned with our shared values and commitment to humanity.

Overview of drones in military operations

DRONES HAVE INCREASINGLY become a pivotal component in modern military operations, transforming how conflicts are managed and fought. Initially developed for reconnaissance purposes, drones have expanded their roles to include surveillance, intelligence gathering, and even direct combat. This evolution has been driven by advancements in technology that allow for more sophisticated aerial vehicles capable of executing complex missions with minimal human intervention. As military organisations around the world adopt these unmanned systems, the strategic implications of their use are profound, altering the landscape of warfare.

The integration of autonomous drone warfare represents a significant shift in military tactics. Drones can operate without direct human control, relying on artificial intelligence to make real-time decisions. This autonomy enables faster response times, particularly in high-stakes environments where every second counts. The use of drones in combat not only reduces the risk to soldiers on the ground but also enhances operational efficiency. The ability to deploy drones for targeted strikes or reconnaissance missions allows militaries to gather intelligence and engage targets with precision, minimising collateral damage and improving mission success rates.

Cyber warfare plays a critical role in the operation of military drones. As these devices rely heavily on data transmission and communication networks, they are vulnerable to cyberattacks. Securing drone operations requires robust cybersecurity measures to protect against hacking and interference. Military organisations must invest in advanced cybersecurity strategies to safeguard their drone fleets and ensure the integrity of the data collected. The intersection of cyber warfare and drone technology highlights the need for ongoing innovation in both fields, as adversaries seek to exploit vulnerabilities in unmanned systems.

The role of advanced robotics in combat extends beyond aerial drones. Ground-based robotic systems are increasingly being utilised for reconnaissance, bomb disposal, and logistical support. These robots can operate in environments that are hazardous for human soldiers, thus preserving lives while performing essential tasks. The integration of augmented reality for tactical training also enhances the effectiveness of military personnel, allowing them to simulate drone operations and understand the complexities of modern warfare in a controlled environment. This training prepares soldiers for real-world scenarios where drones are a critical asset.

As the military looks to the future, the evolution of drone technology will likely intersect with emerging fields such as quantum computing and sustainable energy solutions. Quantum computing could revolutionise data processing speeds for drone operations, allowing for more complex algorithms and quicker decision-making. Meanwhile, sustainable energy solutions will ensure that drone fleets operate with minimal environmental impact. The continuous development of biometric security and identification systems will also enhance operational security, ensuring that only authorised personnel can control or access drone technology. As these advancements unfold, the role of drones in military operations will continue to evolve, shaping the strategies and outcomes of future conflicts.

Advantages and challenges of autonomy

AUTONOMY IN MILITARY operations presents a myriad of advantages that could significantly reshape the landscape of modern warfare. One of the most prominent benefits is the enhancement of operational efficiency. Autonomous systems, such as drones and robotic vehicles, can conduct missions without the immediate presence of human operators, thereby reducing response times and increasing the scope of operations. These systems are capable of processing vast amounts of data quickly, allowing for real-time decision-making that can outpace traditional human-led operations. This efficiency can lead to greater mission success rates and reduced casualties among personnel, as autonomous units can often navigate into hostile environments where human soldiers would face considerable risk.

Moreover, the integration of autonomous technologies fosters improved intelligence gathering and analysis. AI-driven systems can sift through enormous quantities of data—both from the battlefield and cyberspace—allowing military analysts to gain insights that may be missed by human counterparts. This capability not only enhances situational awareness but also supports strategic planning and decision-making. In the context of cyber warfare, autonomous systems can identify and respond to threats at unprecedented speeds, safeguarding critical infrastructure and military networks from potential cyberattacks. This proactive defense mechanism represents a significant shift in how military forces operate in an increasingly digitised world.

However, the transition to a more autonomous military presents notable challenges that must be addressed. One of the primary concerns is the ethical implications of using autonomous systems in combat. The question of accountability arises when an autonomous drone makes a decision that results in collateral damage. Determining who is responsible for such actions—whether it be the commanders who deployed the system, the developers of the technology, or the machine itself—poses a complex moral dilemma. This challenge necessitates the establishment of clear guidelines and regulations governing the use of autonomous weaponry to ensure compliance with international laws and norms.

Another significant challenge lies in the vulnerability of autonomous systems to cyber threats. While they offer enhanced capabilities, these technologies can also be susceptible to hacking and manipulation. Adversaries may exploit weaknesses in software or communication systems, potentially turning an autonomous weapon against its operators. This underscores the importance of robust cybersecurity measures and continuous updates to ensure the integrity and resilience of these systems. As military forces increasingly rely on autonomous technologies, they must also invest in safeguarding them against evolving cyber threats.

Lastly, the implementation of autonomy in warfare raises concerns about the future of human roles within the military. As advanced robotics and AI technologies become more prevalent, there may be fears of job displacement for traditional military personnel. However, rather than replacing human soldiers, these technologies should be viewed as force multipliers that enhance human capabilities. The future military landscape will likely require a new breed of soldier who can effectively collaborate with autonomous systems, leveraging their strengths while maintaining critical decision-making roles. Training and education will be paramount in this transition, ensuring that military personnel are equipped to operate alongside advanced technologies in a rapidly evolving battlefield.

Regulatory and ethical implications

THE INTEGRATION OF advanced technology in military operations has ushered in a new era of warfare, characterized by the increasing reliance on data crafts, autonomous systems, and cyber capabilities. As nations invest in these innovations, regulatory and ethical implications become paramount. The rapid pace of technological advancement often outstrips existing legal frameworks, creating a landscape where compliance and accountability may be challenging to enforce. This dissonance raises critical questions about the governance of such technologies, particularly concerning their deployment in combat scenarios and the potential for unintended consequences.

One significant area of concern is the use of autonomous drones in warfare. As these systems gain capabilities to make decisions without direct human oversight, ethical dilemmas emerge regarding accountability for actions taken in the field. The potential for autonomous drones to engage targets based on algorithms poses risks of misidentification and collateral damage. Regulatory bodies must grapple with establishing guidelines that ensure accountability while balancing operational efficiency and the need for rapid responses on the battlefield. The development of international norms and treaties governing the use of autonomous systems is essential to mitigate risks associated with their deployment.

Cyber warfare further complicates the regulatory landscape, as nations engage in increasingly sophisticated cyber operations. The anonymity and speed of cyber-attacks challenge traditional concepts of sovereignty and warfare. Legal frameworks that govern acts of war may need to evolve to address the unique nature of cyber threats. Issues such as attribution, proportionality, and civilian protection in cyberspace require robust discussions among policymakers, military leaders, and legal experts. The lack of clear regulations can lead to escalatory cycles of retaliation, potentially resulting in widespread conflict without clear boundaries.

The ethical considerations surrounding AI-driven intelligence analysis and decision-making in military operations also demand scrutiny. The incorporation of artificial intelligence in assessing threats and making recommendations can enhance operational effectiveness, yet it raises the specter of biased algorithms leading to unjust outcomes. Ensuring transparency in AI processes and adherence to ethical standards is crucial to maintain public trust and prevent potential abuses. Policymakers must prioritize developing frameworks that guide the ethical use of AI in military contexts, emphasizing fairness, accountability, and respect for human rights.

Lastly, advancements in biometric security and identification technologies present both opportunities and challenges. While these technologies can enhance security and operational efficiency, they also raise concerns regarding privacy and civil liberties. The implementation of biometric systems in military operations necessitates careful consideration of ethical implications, particularly in how personal data is collected, stored, and utilized. Establishing rigorous data protection standards will be vital to foster public trust while ensuring that the military can effectively leverage these technologies in an increasingly complex security environment. As we look to the future of warfare, addressing these regulatory and ethical implications will be essential for fostering responsible innovation in military practices.

87

Chapter 15: Cyber warfare and cybersecurity

Cyber warfare represents a paradigm shift in the landscape of military conflict, where battles are increasingly fought in the digital realm rather than on traditional battlefields. At its core, cyber warfare involves the use of digital attacks by one nation to disrupt the vital computer systems of another, potentially leading to significant physical, economic, and political consequences. This form of warfare leverages advanced technology to exploit vulnerabilities in critical infrastructure, including power grids, financial institutions, and communication networks. As nations become more reliant on interconnected systems, the potential for cyber-attacks to inflict damage grows exponentially, making understanding cyber warfare essential for modern military strategy.

The tactics employed in cyber warfare can range from espionage to sabotage and even psychological operations. Hackers, often state-sponsored, infiltrate systems to steal sensitive information or disrupt services. Such attacks can be executed with relative anonymity, complicating attribution and response efforts. The rise of autonomous systems and AI-driven intelligence analysis has further transformed cyber operations, allowing for rapid data processing and decision-making that outpaces human capabilities. This integration of advanced technologies enhances offensive capabilities and also creates new avenues for defense, as military organizations strive to protect their networks from increasingly sophisticated threats.

In the context of military operations, cyber warfare is not merely an auxiliary component; it is a central element of modern combat strategies. The ability to incapacitate an enemy's command and control systems can provide a decisive advantage in a conflict. Moreover, cyber warfare can be conducted in conjunction with traditional military tactics, blurring the lines between physical and digital battles. As advanced robotics and autonomous drones are deployed in combat, the interconnectivity of these systems with cyber capabilities becomes increasingly important. Ensuring that these platforms are secure from cyber threats is crucial for maintaining operational integrity.

Augmented reality (AR) is emerging as a valuable tool for training military personnel in cyber warfare. Through immersive simulations, soldiers can gain hands-on experience in identifying and responding to cyber threats. This training is vital, given the rapid evolution of technology and the ongoing arms race in cyber capabilities. Furthermore, wearable technology enhances situational awareness, allowing soldiers to receive real-time updates on potential cyber threats. As the military seeks to integrate these innovative technologies, the emphasis on cybersecurity becomes paramount, requiring ongoing investment and adaptation to evolving threats.

Looking to the future, the implications of cyber warfare extend beyond immediate military applications. The intersection of quantum computing and cybersecurity presents both opportunities and challenges, as quantum technologies have the potential to create unbreakable encryption while also enabling sophisticated cyber-attacks. Additionally, as military operations increasingly depend on space-based defense systems, protecting these assets from cyber threats becomes essential. The evolution of biometrics for security and identification further underscores the need for robust cybersecurity measures. As we navigate this new age of warfare, understanding cyber warfare is critical for governments, military leaders, and the public to ensure resilience against emerging threats and to safeguard national security.

Key cyber threats to national security

THE LANDSCAPE OF NATIONAL security is increasingly shaped by cyber threats that exploit vulnerabilities in technology and infrastructure. As nations become more reliant on digital systems for communication, intelligence, and operational capabilities, the potential for cyberattacks to disrupt critical functions grows. Adversaries can employ a range of tactics, from sophisticated hacking techniques to the deployment of malware, aiming to steal sensitive information, compromise military operations, or even manipulate public perception. The implications of such threats extend beyond immediate damage, potentially destabilising entire governments and undermining trust in national institutions.

One of the most pressing concerns involves state-sponsored cyber warfare, where nation-states engage in hostile activities against each other through cyber means. This form of warfare can manifest in various ways, including espionage, sabotage, and the dissemination of disinformation. For example, hacking into military databases can yield strategic advantages, allowing adversaries to gain insights into troop movements or operational plans. Additionally, the use of social media platforms for misinformation campaigns can influence public opinion and create societal discord, demonstrating that the cyber battlefield often extends into the realm of psychological operations.

Cybersecurity measures remain a critical component of safeguarding national interests. As militaries adopt advanced technologies such as autonomous drones and AI-driven intelligence systems, the need for robust cybersecurity protocols becomes paramount. Vulnerabilities in these systems can be exploited, potentially rendering them ineffective during critical operations. The integration of biometric security and identification methods offers a promising avenue for enhancing security, ensuring that only authorised personnel can access sensitive information and systems. However, as technology evolves, so too must the strategies employed to defend against emerging cyber threats.

The interplay between cyber capabilities and advanced technologies like quantum computing is also noteworthy. Quantum computing holds the potential to revolutionise data processing and encryption, which can be both a boon and a bane for national security. While it could enhance security measures through superior encryption techniques, it also poses a threat as adversaries may develop quantum capabilities to break existing encryption methods. This duality necessitates a forward-thinking approach to military strategy, where proactive measures are taken to stay ahead of adversarial advancements in technology.

Lastly, the increasing reliance on space-based defense systems introduces another dimension to the cyber threat landscape. As nations deploy satellites for communication, surveillance, and navigation, these systems become prime targets for cyberattacks. Disrupting satellite operations could incapacitate military forces and civilian infrastructure alike, demonstrating the interconnectedness of cyber warfare and traditional military operations. To address these threats, nations must prioritise the development of comprehensive cybersecurity frameworks that encompass all facets of military operations, ensuring resilience against an ever-evolving array of cyber threats to national security.

Strategies for cyber defense

IN THE EVOLVING LANDSCAPE of modern warfare, effective strategies for cyber defense are essential to protect military operations from increasingly sophisticated cyber threats. As the integration of advanced technologies such as autonomous drones, artificial intelligence, and quantum computing becomes prevalent, the military must prioritise the development of robust cyber defenses. This entails not only safeguarding critical infrastructure and sensitive data but also ensuring that communication networks are resilient against potential intrusions and attacks.

One of the primary strategies for enhancing cyber defense is the implementation of a layered security model. This approach involves multiple defensive measures that work together to create a comprehensive security architecture. By deploying firewalls, intrusion detection systems, and endpoint protection solutions, military organisations can fortify their networks against various types of cyber threats. Additionally, the use of encryption technologies can protect data in transit and at rest, making it significantly more difficult for adversaries to access or exploit sensitive information.

Training and awareness are also crucial components of effective cyber defense strategies. As personnel increasingly rely on advanced technologies and digital platforms, it is imperative to equip them with the knowledge and skills needed to recognise and respond to cyber threats. Regular training programs that simulate real-world cyber-attack scenarios can help military personnel develop critical thinking and decision-making capabilities in the face of cyber incidents. Fostering a culture of cybersecurity awareness within the military organization can significantly reduce the likelihood of human error, which remains a common vulnerability in cyber defense.

Incorporating advanced technologies such as artificial intelligence and machine learning into cyber defense strategies can enhance threat detection and response capabilities. AI-driven systems can analyze vast amounts of data in real-time, identifying patterns and anomalies that may indicate a cyber threat.

92

Chapter 16: Advanced robotics in combat

Military robots have evolved significantly, serving various roles in modern warfare. These machines can be broadly categorised into several types, each designed to meet specific operational needs. The most common types include unmanned aerial vehicles (UAVs), ground robots, and maritime drones. UAVs are perhaps the most recognisable, often used for reconnaissance, surveillance, and air strikes. Equipped with advanced sensors and cameras, they provide real-time intelligence to military commanders, enabling better decision-making on the battlefield. Ground robots, on the other hand, are designed for tasks such as bomb disposal, logistics support, and reconnaissance missions. These robots can navigate challenging terrains and perform dangerous tasks without risking human lives. Maritime drones, while less prominent, play a critical role in naval warfare, capable of conducting surveillance, reconnaissance, and even engaging enemy vessels.

Autonomous systems represent a significant advancement in military robotics. These robots are equipped with artificial intelligence, allowing them to operate independently without direct human control. They can analyze vast amounts of data, make decisions in real-time, and adapt to changing battlefield conditions. Autonomous drones, for instance, can carry out complex missions such as target acquisition, enemy tracking, and even engaging adversarial forces. This capability enhances operational efficiency and reduces the cognitive burden on human operators. However, the deployment of autonomous systems raises ethical and accountability concerns, prompting discussions about the need for regulations governing their use in combat situations.

In addition to combat roles, military robots are increasingly utilised for training and simulation. Augmented reality (AR) technology is being integrated into training programs to create immersive environments for soldiers. AR can simulate combat scenarios, allowing troops to practice their skills in a controlled setting. This technology enhances training effectiveness and also helps in familiarising soldiers with advanced robotic systems they may encounter in the field. Furthermore, wearable technology is being developed to provide soldiers with real-time data and analytics, improving their situational awareness and decision-making capabilities during operations.

Another area where military robots have a significant impact is in intelligence gathering and cybersecurity. AI-driven intelligence analysis tools sift through massive datasets to identify patterns and anomalies that may indicate threats. These systems enhance situational awareness and support proactive measures to counter potential cyber threats. As cyber warfare becomes increasingly prominent, the integration of advanced robotics and AI in cybersecurity efforts is essential. Biometric security systems are also being developed to ensure the integrity of military operations, utilising facial recognition and other biometric data to identify personnel and secure sensitive areas.

Looking ahead, the future of military robots is intertwined with innovations in quantum computing and sustainable energy solutions. Quantum computing holds the potential to revolutionize military strategy by enabling faster data processing and more sophisticated simulations of complex combat scenarios. Additionally, sustainable energy solutions are being explored to power military operations, reducing reliance on traditional fuel sources and lowering the environmental impact of warfare. As these technologies continue to advance, the role of robots in military operations will expand, shaping the landscape of future conflicts and enhancing the effectiveness of armed forces around the world.

Integration of robotics in tactical operations

THE INTEGRATION OF robotics in tactical operations marks a transformative shift in modern warfare, leveraging advanced technologies to enhance combat effectiveness and operational efficiency

Autonomous drone warfare represents a significant evolution in military operations. Drones can survey vast areas, gather intelligence, and execute precision strikes with minimal human intervention. The ability to operate in contested environments without risking pilot lives has made drones a staple in modern combat scenarios. These aerial vehicles are equipped with advanced sensors and AI-driven analytics that allow them to process data in real time, making them invaluable for reconnaissance missions and targeted attacks. As the technology continues to advance, we can expect drones to become even more autonomous, capable of making decisions based on their programming and environmental assessments.

In conjunction with drone technology, robotics also plays a crucial role in augmenting ground operations. Autonomous ground vehicles can be utilised for logistics, reconnaissance, and even direct combat roles, reducing the burden on personnel and allowing human soldiers to focus on higher-level strategic tasks. These vehicles can navigate complex terrains, interact with their environment, and even collaborate with other robotic systems, creating a networked force that operates seamlessly.

The intersection of robotics and augmented reality further enriches tactical training for military personnel. By integrating advanced simulation technologies, soldiers can engage in realistic training scenarios that incorporate robotic systems. This immersive approach enables troops to understand how to effectively collaborate with robotic assets in real-world situations. Moreover, augmented reality can provide real-time data overlays during missions, enhancing situational awareness and decision-making processes. As soldiers become more accustomed to working alongside robots, the potential for improved outcomes in live operations increases significantly.

The future of warfare will inevitably intertwine robotics with other technological advancements, such as AI-driven intelligence analysis and quantum computing. The ability to analyze vast amounts of data quickly and accurately will inform tactical decisions and enhance strategic planning. Robotics will also play a critical role in cybersecurity, providing defense against potential threats to military infrastructure. As these technologies converge, the integration of robotics in tactical operations will not only redefine how conflicts are fought but also reshape global military strategies, leading to a new era of warfare characterized by precision, efficiency, and a reduced human footprint on the battlefield.

Future trends in military robotics

THE FUTURE OF MILITARY robotics is poised to be transformative, driven by advancements in technology that promise to redefine the battlefield landscape. As nations invest in research and development, we can expect an increase in the deployment of autonomous systems that enhance operational efficiency and effectiveness. These robots will not only perform routine tasks but also engage in complex decision-making processes, significantly reducing the cognitive load on human operators. By integrating artificial intelligence, military robotics will enable faster response times and improved strategic planning, thereby altering the dynamics of warfare.

One of the most significant trends in military robotics is the expansion of drone warfare. Autonomous drones equipped with advanced sensors and AI capabilities are expected to play a crucial role in intelligence-gathering, surveillance, and even combat missions. These drones can operate in environments too dangerous for human soldiers, providing real-time data and facilitating precision strikes with minimal collateral damage. As drone technology continues to evolve, we may see the emergence of swarming tactics, where fleets of drones can coordinate their actions autonomously to overwhelm enemy defenses, creating new challenges for airspace management and countermeasures.

Cyber warfare and cybersecurity are increasingly intertwined with developments in military robotics. As autonomous systems become more prevalent, the potential for cyberattacks on these technologies grows significantly. Future military robotics will need to incorporate robust cybersecurity measures to protect against hacking and manipulation. This will require a new level of collaboration between roboticists and cybersecurity experts to ensure that systems are resilient to threats. Furthermore, the integration of AI-driven intelligence analysis will enhance the ability to predict and respond to cyber threats, providing a strategic advantage in the digital domain of warfare.

Augmented reality is set to revolutionize tactical training for soldiers, integrating advanced robotics into simulation environments. By using augmented reality, military personnel can practice their skills in realistic settings without the risks associated with live training exercises. This technology allows for the modeling of various combat scenarios, enabling soldiers to interact with robotic systems in a controlled environment. As training becomes more sophisticated, soldiers will develop a deeper understanding of how to effectively work alongside autonomous systems, fostering a seamless human-robot collaboration on the battlefield.

Looking ahead, the integration of quantum computing into military strategy could further enhance the capabilities of robotic systems. Quantum computing offers the potential for unprecedented processing power, enabling complex simulations and data analysis at speeds currently unattainable. This could lead to breakthroughs in decision-making algorithms for autonomous robots, allowing for real-time adaptations to dynamic battlefield conditions. As nations race to harness quantum technology, the implications for military robotics will be profound, potentially shifting the balance of power in future conflicts and redefining the nature of warfare itself.

Chapter 17: Augmented reality for tactical training

The role of AR in military training

The integration of augmented reality (AR) into military training represents a significant leap forward in preparing armed forces for modern warfare. AR technology enhances training environments by overlaying digital information onto the physical world, allowing soldiers to engage in realistic simulations that mimic combat scenarios without the risks associated with traditional live training exercises. This immersive experience enables personnel to practice skills such as navigation, tactical decision-making, and teamwork in a controlled setting, ultimately improving their readiness for real-world operations.

One of the key benefits of AR in military training is its ability to provide instant feedback and adaptive learning experiences. Trainees can receive real-time assessments of their performance, allowing them to identify weaknesses and improve their skills on the spot. Instructors can also utilize AR to create complex scenarios that evolve based on the actions of the trainees, fostering critical thinking and adaptability in unpredictable environments. This iterative learning process is vital as modern conflicts often require rapid adjustments and innovative strategies.

AR can facilitate remote training, enabling soldiers to participate in exercises from various locations. This capability is particularly advantageous for units stationed in different parts of the world or during times when travel is restricted due to budgetary constraints or safety concerns. By using AR technology, military leaders can ensure that all personnel receive consistent training experiences, regardless of geographical limitations, thus maintaining a high level of operational readiness across the force.

In addition to enhancing individual skills, AR fosters collaboration among units by simulating joint operations. Through shared AR platforms, different branches of the military can train together, enhancing their ability to coordinate efforts in real combat situations. This collaborative training is essential, as modern warfare often involves multiple domains, including land, air, and cyber, requiring seamless integration among different military components. As units gain familiarity with each other's roles and capabilities through AR training, the likelihood of successful joint operations increases.

As augmented reality continues to evolve, its applications in military training are likely to expand even further. Future advancements may include the incorporation of artificial intelligence to create more sophisticated training scenarios that adapt dynamically to the trainees' decisions and actions. Furthermore, it can be argued that the integration of AR with wearable technology could provide soldiers with real-time data and analytics during training exercises, offering insights that enhance both individual and unit performance. As military training evolves to meet the demands of future combat environments, AR will undoubtedly play a crucial role in shaping the next generation of prepared and resilient armed forces.

Benefits of immersive learning environments

IMMERSIVE LEARNING environments are revolutionizing training and operational strategies within the military, particularly in the context of future warfare. These environments utilise advanced technologies such as virtual reality (VR), augmented reality (AR), and simulation systems to create realistic scenarios that allow soldiers to engage in comprehensive training exercises. By immersing personnel in lifelike situations, these environments enhance skill acquisition, decision-making, and teamwork, ultimately preparing military forces for the complexities of modern combat.

Case studies of AR implementation

IN RECENT YEARS, AUGMENTED reality (AR) has emerged as a transformative technology within military operations, enhancing training, situational awareness, and decision-making processes. One prominent example of AR application is the U.S. Army's Integrated Visual Augmentation System (IVAS). This system integrates AR capabilities with advanced headsets to provide soldiers with a comprehensive view of their surroundings. By overlaying critical information such as enemy positions, terrain data, and navigation aids onto the soldier's field of vision, IVAS significantly enhances situational awareness, allowing troops to make informed decisions rapidly in dynamic combat environments.

Another noteworthy case study is the use of AR by the U.S. Marine Corps for tactical training exercises. The Marines have implemented AR solutions that simulate real-world scenarios, allowing soldiers to engage in realistic combat training without the logistical challenges of traditional exercises. These AR simulations can mimic various environmental conditions and enemy tactics, providing a safe yet effective training platform. By utilising AR, the Marines can enhance their readiness and adaptability, ensuring that soldiers are better prepared for the unpredictability of modern warfare.

The British Army has also explored AR technology through its use in command-and-control operations. By employing AR overlays, commanders are able to visualize battlefield dynamics in real-time, facilitating improved communication and coordination among units. This application of AR aids in immediate tactical decisions and also allows for post-mission analysis, where commanders can review engagements and refine strategies based on a clearer understanding of the events that unfolded. Such enhancements are crucial in an age where timely and accurate information can mean the difference between mission success and failure.

In the realm of cybersecurity, AR is being leveraged to improve the training of personnel tasked with defending against cyber threats. The NATO Cyber Defense Centre of Excellence has developed AR-based training modules that simulate cyber-attack scenarios, providing operators with immersive experiences to hone their skills. This innovative approach to training allows cybersecurity professionals to practice their response to various threats in a controlled environment, ultimately leading to more effective defense strategies in real-world situations.

Lastly, the integration of wearable AR technology in soldier equipment is becoming increasingly prevalent. The U.S. Army's Program Executive Office Soldier is developing AR-enabled headsets that provide soldiers with real-time data feeds, including health metrics and environmental information. This wearable technology not only enhances individual soldier performance but also contributes to the overall operational effectiveness of military units.

Chapter 18: AI-Driven intelligence and analysis

AI technologies are revolutionising military intelligence, offering unprecedented capabilities that enhance decision-making and operational efficiency. The integration of artificial intelligence into military operations enables the analysis of vast amounts of data at speeds and accuracies far beyond human capabilities. This data-driven approach allows for more informed strategic planning and real-time assessments of situations on the battlefield. Leveraging machine learning algorithms and advanced analytics, military intelligence can predict potential threats and identify patterns that were previously invisible, leading to proactive measures rather than reactive responses.

One of the most significant advancements in military intelligence is the development of AI-driven intelligence analysis tools. These systems can sift through massive datasets, including satellite imagery, communications intercepts, and social media activity, to extract actionable insights. For instance, AI algorithms can analyse imagery to detect changes in enemy installations or troop movements, providing commanders with critical information that can influence tactical decisions. This capability improves situational awareness and also enhances the military's ability to anticipate and counter adversarial actions in real time.

Autonomous drone warfare exemplifies another area where AI technologies are making a profound impact. Drones equipped with AI can conduct surveillance, reconnaissance, and targeted strikes with minimal human intervention. These unmanned aerial vehicles are capable of processing data onboard, allowing them to adapt to changing environments and make split-second decisions during missions. The use of AI in drone operations not increases operational efficiency and also reduces the risk to human pilots, thereby changing the dynamics of aerial combat and intelligence-gathering missions.

Cyber warfare and cybersecurity also benefit significantly from advancements in AI technologies. With the growing complexity of cyber threats, military intelligence agencies employ AI systems to detect and respond to potential breaches more effectively. These systems utilize machine learning to identify unusual patterns in network traffic, enabling rapid responses to cyber-attacks. Furthermore, AI can assist in developing robust defense mechanisms, ensuring that military operations can continue uninterrupted in the face of increasingly sophisticated cyber threats.

Enhancing Decision-making with AI

ENHANCING DECISION-making with artificial intelligence (AI) represents a pivotal transformation in the way military operations are conducted in the modern landscape of warfare. The integration of AI into military decision-making processes allows for more efficient data analysis and real-time insights that can significantly improve operational outcomes. By leveraging vast amounts of data collected from various sources, including reconnaissance, intelligence reports, and battlefield sensors, AI can assist commanders in identifying patterns and making informed decisions faster than traditional methods would allow. This capability is essential in dynamic combat environments where timely and accurate decision-making can be the difference between success and failure.

AI-driven intelligence analysis is one of the most impactful applications of artificial intelligence in military contexts. By employing machine learning algorithms, military analysts can automate the interpretation of complex data sets, enabling them to focus on strategic tasks rather than labour-intensive data sifting. This technology enhances situational awareness by providing predictive analytics that can forecast enemy movements, assess potential threats, and evaluate mission outcomes. The ability to process and analise data at unprecedented speeds allows military leaders to adapt strategies in real-time, ensuring they remain one step ahead of adversaries.

In addition to intelligence analysis, AI plays a critical role in optimising logistics and resource management on the battlefield. Autonomous systems, such as drones and robotic vehicles, equipped with AI capabilities, can efficiently manage supply chains, monitor equipment status, and execute resupply missions with minimal human intervention. This not only streamlines operations but also reduces the risk to personnel in hostile environments. As military engagements increasingly rely on sophisticated technology, the ability to integrate AI into logistics and support operations becomes essential for maintaining operational readiness and effectiveness.

henceforth, augmented reality (AR) systems powered by AI contribute to enhanced tactical training for soldiers. By simulating real-world combat scenarios, AR can provide immersive training experiences that adapt to individual soldiers' performance and learning curves. AI can analyse trainees' actions and decisions in real-time, offering personalised feedback and recommendations that improve their skills and readiness for actual combat situations. This advanced training approach ensures that military personnel are not only familiar with their equipment but are also adept at making quick, informed decisions under pressure.

Finally, the future of warfare will increasingly rely on AI to manage cybersecurity threats and protect critical military infrastructure. As cyber warfare becomes a more significant element of military strategy, AI systems can detect and respond to cyber threats more effectively than human operators alone. By continuously monitoring network traffic and identifying anomalies, AI can provide early warnings of potential breaches and enable rapid countermeasures. In an era where information dominance is crucial, the ability to safeguard sensitive data and maintain operational security is paramount, underscoring the importance of AI in enhancing decision-making processes in military operations.

Challenges in AI implementation

THE INTEGRATION OF artificial intelligence (AI) into military operations presents numerous challenges that must be navigated to harness its potential effectively. For one, the rapid pace of technological advancement often outstrips the ability of military organisations to adapt their strategies and protocols accordingly. As AI technologies evolve, so too must the frameworks governing their use, ensuring that ethical considerations, legal standards, and operational guidelines are kept current. This ongoing lag can hinder the operational readiness of armed forces that seek to implement AI-driven solutions, particularly in areas like autonomous drone warfare and advanced robotics in combat.

Data quality and availability represent another significant hurdle in AI implementation. Military operations rely heavily on accurate, timely data to make informed decisions, and AI systems are only as good as the data fed into them. Inconsistent data sources, incomplete datasets, and the challenge of integrating diverse data streams can lead to unreliable AI outputs. This issue is particularly pertinent in intelligence analysis and cyber warfare, where the stakes are high, and the margin for error is slim. Ensuring robust data collection and management processes is essential for the success of AI applications in the military domain.

Cybersecurity concerns further complicate the landscape of AI implementation. As military systems incorporate AI, they become increasingly interconnected, which can expose them to new vulnerabilities. The potential for cyberattacks on AI systems raises critical questions about the robustness of these technologies in hostile environments. Protecting AI-driven platforms, such as those used in biometric security and identification or space-based defense systems, requires ongoing vigilance and sophisticated cybersecurity measures. The challenge lies not only in defending against external threats but also in ensuring the integrity of the data these systems rely on.

Another challenge is the need for extensive training and adaptation among military personnel. Implementing AI systems involves a steep learning curve, necessitating that soldiers and commanders alike become proficient with new technologies. This requirement extends beyond technical skills; it also includes understanding the implications of AI in combat scenarios, including ethical considerations and potential biases inherent in AI algorithms. The integration of augmented reality for tactical training can help bridge this gap, providing immersive learning experiences that prepare personnel for AI-enhanced operational environments.

The reliance on autonomous systems raises questions about accountability in combat situations. Who is responsible when an AI system makes a decision that leads to civilian casualties or fails to engage a legitimate threat? Developing clear policies and ethical guidelines for AI use in military settings is crucial to addressing these concerns. The balance between leveraging advanced technologies for strategic advantages and adhering to humanitarian laws and ethical standards remains a fundamental challenge that must be confronted as the military continues to navigate the complexities of AI implementation.

Chapter 19: Wearable technology for soldiers

Wearable devices in combat represent a significant shift in military technology, enhancing the capabilities of soldiers on the battlefield. These devices range from smart helmets and augmented reality visors to biometric sensors and health monitoring systems. The integration of wearable technology allows for real-time data collection and analysis, which can be crucial in dynamic combat environments. As soldiers engage in increasingly complex operations, the ability to access vital information instantly can mean the difference between mission success and failure.

One of the primary advantages of wearable devices is their ability to enhance situational awareness. For example, augmented reality headsets can overlay critical data directly onto a soldier's field of vision, providing information about enemy positions, terrain, and mission objectives without the need to refer to traditional maps or manuals. This integration of information allows for quicker decision-making and improved coordination among units. The real-time updates also facilitate better communication and teamwork, as soldiers can share vital information instantaneously, enhancing operational effectiveness.

Wearable technology also plays a crucial role in monitoring the health and well-being of soldiers. Biometric sensors can track vital signs such as heart rate, body temperature, and stress levels, providing commanders with a better understanding of their troops' physical and mental states. This data can be used to make informed decisions about troop deployment and to identify when a soldier may be experiencing fatigue or stress that could impair performance. By incorporating health monitoring into wearable devices, the military can enhance soldier resilience and readiness for prolonged engagements.

Wearable devices can assist in data collection and analysis for strategic planning. With advancements in artificial intelligence, these devices can analyze patterns in soldier performance and environmental conditions, offering insights that can improve future operations.

Impact on soldier health and performance

THE INTEGRATION OF advanced technologies in modern warfare has a profound impact on soldier health and performance. As military operations increasingly leverage skiving data crafts and autonomous systems, the physical and mental demands placed on soldiers are evolving. Soldiers must adapt to new combat environments characterised by rapid data processing, sophisticated AI-driven intelligence analysis, and augmented reality training. These advancements not only change the way soldiers are trained and equipped but also influence their overall well-being and effectiveness on the battlefield.

Wearable technology plays a crucial role in monitoring soldier health in real-time. Devices equipped with biometric sensors can track vital signs, fatigue levels, and stress indicators, providing commanders with valuable data to assess a soldier's readiness. This continuous health monitoring can lead to timely interventions, ensuring that soldiers do not operate beyond their physical limits.

The psychological impact of warfare is also evolving with the introduction of advanced robotics and AI. Soldiers may face unique mental health challenges arising from interactions with autonomous systems, including feelings of isolation or detachment. The reliance on cyber warfare tactics can create stress due to the high stakes of digital security and the potential for cyber attacks on personal and military infrastructure. Training programs that incorporate augmented reality can help soldiers prepare for these challenges, providing immersive experiences that simulate the complexities of modern combat. By addressing both physical and mental health, military organisations can cultivate resilience in their ranks.

Quantum computing is set to revolutionise military strategy, but its implications for soldier performance must not be overlooked. As data processing speeds increase, the potential for real-time decision-making enhances the effectiveness of military operations. However, the rapid pace of change may overwhelm soldiers who are required to adapt to new systems and processes. Continuous training and support are essential to ensure that soldiers can leverage these advancements without compromising their mental well-being. A focus on sustainable energy solutions is necessary because of the importance of maintaining soldier health, as a well-supported logistics framework reduces the burden on troops in the field.

The future of warfare necessitates a holistic approach to soldier health and performance. Emphasising physical fitness, mental resilience, and the effective use of technology will be critical in preparing military personnel for the challenges ahead. As the landscape of combat continues to evolve with innovations in space-based defense systems and biometric security, a proactive stance on soldier health will not only enhance individual performance but also contribute to the overall success of military operations. By prioritising the well-being of soldiers, military organisations can ensure they are equipped to face the demands of future battles.

Future developments in wearable tech

WEARABLE TECHNOLOGY has rapidly evolved, becoming an integral part of modern military operations. As we look toward the future, the advancements in this field promise to enhance the capabilities of soldiers on the battlefield significantly. The next generation of wearable devices will not only focus on health and fitness tracking but also integrate advanced functionality such as real-time data analysis, environmental monitoring, and enhanced communication systems. These devices will be designed to provide soldiers with crucial information at their fingertips, facilitating quicker decision-making in high-stakes situations.

One of the most exciting prospects is the integration of augmented reality (AR) into wearable tech. Future headsets may allow soldiers to visualize battlefield data overlaying their real-world view, providing insights such as troop movements, enemy positions, and tactical advantages. This technology could lead to improved situational awareness, enabling forces to react swiftly and strategically. Additionally, AR could be used for training purposes, creating immersive environments that simulate combat scenarios, thereby enhancing soldiers' preparedness without the risks associated with live training exercises.

Biometric capabilities in wearable technology will also see significant advancements. Future devices are expected to include integrated biometric sensors that can monitor a soldier's vital signs in real-time, detecting stress levels, fatigue, or potential injuries. This data can be crucial for commanders, allowing them to make informed decisions regarding troop deployment and health management. Moreover, the integration of biometric identification systems will enhance security, ensuring that only authorised personnel can access sensitive information or equipment, thereby mitigating risks associated with infiltration or espionage.

As cyber warfare continues to pose threats to military operations, the future of wearable technology will also prioritise cybersecurity. Wearable devices will need to be equipped with robust encryption and security protocols to protect sensitive data from cyber-attacks. Ensuring that these devices are resilient against hacking attempts will be critical, as compromised technology could lead to catastrophic failures in communication or decision-making during missions. The emphasis on cybersecurity within wearable tech development will be essential in maintaining operational integrity and safeguarding military assets.

Chapter 20: Quantum computing in military strategy

Quantum computing represents a significant departure from traditional computing, harnessing the principles of quantum mechanics to process information in ways that were previously unimaginable. At its core, quantum computing employs qubits, which can exist in multiple states simultaneously, unlike classical bits that are strictly binary. This unique characteristic allows quantum computers to perform complex calculations at extraordinary speeds, making them particularly well-suited for tasks such as cryptography, optimisation, and simulations that are critical in military applications.

In the context of military strategy, quantum computing holds the potential to revolutionise data analysis and decision-making processes. Advanced algorithms can leverage the power of quantum computing to sift through vast amounts of intelligence data, identifying patterns and anomalies that would be nearly impossible for classical systems to detect. This capability can enhance situational awareness for military commanders, enabling them to make informed decisions based on real-time information, ultimately improving operational effectiveness on the battlefield.

The ability to break traditional encryption methods poses a threat to sensitive military communications and data. However, quantum computing also offers the potential for developing unbreakable encryption methods, such as quantum key distribution, which could safeguard military communications against cyber threats. As adversaries increasingly turn to cyber warfare tactics, the military must adapt by integrating quantum technologies into their cybersecurity frameworks to protect vital information.

Quantum computing extend beyond data analysis and cybersecurity; they also influence the design of advanced autonomous systems. By incorporating quantum algorithms, military drones and robotics can improve decision-making capabilities, maneuverability, and mission efficiency. This integration can lead to the development of autonomous systems that are not only faster but also more adaptable to changing battlefield conditions, enhancing the military's operational capabilities in complex environments.

As nations race to harness the potential of quantum computing, the military must prioritise investments in research and development to remain competitive. Establishing partnerships with technology firms, academic institutions, and research organisations will be essential to drive innovation in this field. Of course, there must be trust on those exposed to projects etc. mind you we do have people in universities who are not nationals and do not fall under a country's laws however, trust on these advanced research undertakings must be paramount. So, as quantum technologies evolve, they will play a pivotal role in shaping the future of warfare, influencing everything from strategy and tactics to the very nature of conflict itself. The integration of quantum computing into military operations will undoubtedly create new paradigms of power and security in the evolving landscape of global warfare.

The integration of advanced technologies into military operations presents a transformative potential that could redefine modern warfare. Skiving data crafts, which leverage data manipulation and tactics to evade detection, could significantly enhance stealth capabilities for military assets. These crafts can operate under the radar by continuously adapting their signatures and routes based on real-time data analysis, making them invaluable for reconnaissance missions. Their ability to analyse enemy movements and predict potential threats while remaining undetected can lead to a strategic advantage in both offensive and defensive operations.

Autonomous drone warfare represents another frontier in military operations. Drones equipped with artificial intelligence can execute complex missions without direct human control, allowing for rapid response to emerging threats. These unmanned systems can conduct surveillance, deliver payloads, and perform precision strikes with minimal risk to personnel. The use of autonomous drones increases operational efficiency and also reduces the likelihood of casualties, fundamentally changing the calculus of engagement in hostile environments.

The incorporation of wearable technology and biometric security systems can further improve military operations. Wearable devices can monitor soldiers' health metrics and performance, ensuring they are physically and mentally prepared for combat. Biometric identification methods enhance security protocols, allowing for efficient access control to sensitive areas and information. Additionally, the advent of quantum computing could revolutionize military strategy by enabling rapid processing of vast amounts of data for intelligence analysis and logistics planning. Together, these innovations will foster a more agile and responsive military force capable of adapting to the ever-changing landscape of warfare.

Implications for security and strategy

THE EVOLVING LANDSCAPE of warfare, shaped by advancements in technology, necessitates a reevaluation of security strategies and military operations. As skiving data crafts emerge as a pivotal element in modern combat, their implications extend beyond traditional battlefield tactics.

The implications for security are profound, as these systems can be vulnerable to cyber-attacks, potentially allowing adversaries to hijack or disable critical assets. Military strategies must therefore incorporate robust cybersecurity measures to safeguard autonomous systems, ensuring that their deployment enhances operational effectiveness rather than creating new vulnerabilities.

The rise of advanced robotics in combat scenarios introduces another layer of complexity. Robots can perform tasks that are too dangerous for human soldiers, but their effectiveness is contingent upon reliable communication and data integrity. As reliance on robotics increases, so too does the importance of securing communication channels against enemy interference. This necessitates a comprehensive approach to cybersecurity, integrating biometric security and identification measures to ensure that only authorised personnel can interact with these systems. The strategic implications are clear: maintaining technological superiority will depend on a proactive stance towards both development and protection of robotic assets.

Augmented reality for tactical training is revolutionising how soldiers prepare for combat. By providing immersive training environments that simulate real-world scenarios, augmented reality enhances decision-making skills and situational awareness. However, this technology also presents security challenges, particularly in safeguarding sensitive training data from cyber intrusions. Military strategies must account for these vulnerabilities by implementing rigorous cybersecurity protocols and ensuring that personnel are trained to recognise and mitigate potential threats in both training and operational environments.

Looking to the future, the integration of quantum computing into military strategy holds the potential to transform data processing and encryption capabilities. The ability to analyze vast amounts of information instantaneously could enhance AI-driven intelligence analysis, enabling faster and more accurate threat assessments. However, this power also necessitates a reevaluation of current security measures, as quantum computing could render traditional encryption methods obsolete. As military operations increasingly rely on cutting-edge technologies, developing sustainable energy solutions to support these advancements becomes essential, ensuring that the military can operate efficiently and effectively in diverse environments. The implications for security and strategy are profound, demanding an adaptive approach that embraces innovation while addressing the associated risks.

Chapter 21: Space-based defense systems

Overview of Space Warfare

Space warfare represents a critical frontier in the evolution of military strategy and technology, driven by the increasing reliance on space-based assets for national security. As nations expand their capabilities in space, the potential for conflict beyond Earth's atmosphere is reaching unprecedented levels. The strategic importance of satellites for communication, navigation, reconnaissance, and missile warning systems means that they are essential to modern military operations. As such, securing these assets against threats, both physical and cyber, has become a priority for many countries, highlighting the need for a comprehensive understanding of space warfare dynamics.

The aspects of space warfare encompass various technologies and strategies, including the deployment of anti-satellite weapons and the development of space-based defense systems. Countries are investing in capabilities that can disrupt or destroy enemy satellites, which can have crippling effects on the adversary's military operations. This includes kinetic options, such as missiles designed to target satellites, as well as non-kinetic methods like electronic warfare aimed at jamming communications. The emergence of such technologies raises ethical and strategic questions about the rules of engagement in space and the potential for escalation of conflicts.

In addition to physical weapons, cyber warfare plays a significant role in space operations. As satellites become increasingly interconnected and reliant on ground-based systems, the threat of cyber-attacks grows. Adversaries may exploit vulnerabilities in satellite software and hardware to disrupt services or gain unauthorised access to sensitive information. This intertwining of cyber warfare and space operations necessitates a robust cybersecurity framework to protect space assets. Consequently, military strategies must integrate cyber defense measures with traditional space warfare tactics to safeguard national interests.

The future of space warfare will also be shaped by advancements in technologies such as artificial intelligence, robotics, and augmented reality. AI-driven intelligence analysis can enhance situational awareness and decision-making processes in space operations, allowing for quicker responses to potential threats. Autonomous drones and robotic systems may be deployed for reconnaissance missions or even as offensive tools, providing capabilities that reduce the risk to human personnel. Furthermore, augmented reality can be utilised for tactical training, enabling soldiers to simulate space combat environments and improve their readiness for potential engagements.

As nations navigate the complexities of space warfare, considerations of sustainability and ethical implications will become increasingly important. The militarization of space carries with it the risk of space debris and environmental impact, prompting discussions on sustainable energy solutions for military operations in space. As we move into this new age of warfare, understanding the multifaceted nature of space warfare will be essential for policymakers, military leaders, and the public alike.

Current technologies in space defense

CURRENT TECHNOLOGIES in space defense are becoming increasingly vital as nations recognise the strategic importance of securing their interests in outer space. As satellite systems are essential for communication, navigation, and intelligence, they are also vulnerable to a range of threats, from anti-satellite weapons to cyber-attacks. Governments are investing heavily in space-based defense systems to protect these assets, developing technologies that can detect, track, and neutralise potential threats in orbit. This includes the deployment of advanced sensors and surveillance systems that can monitor space debris and hostile activities, ensuring that critical infrastructure remains operational and secure.

In addition to traditional surveillance, autonomous drone warfare is making its mark in the realm of space defense. Unmanned aerial vehicles (UAVs) equipped with sophisticated payloads can be deployed to monitor potential threats, collect intelligence, or even engage in combat scenarios. These drones can operate in tandem with satellite systems, providing real-time data that enhances situational awareness. The incorporation of artificial intelligence into drone operations allows for rapid decision-making and adaptive responses to evolving threats, making them invaluable assets in the defense of space.

Future of military operations in space

THE FUTURE OF MILITARY operations in space is set to transform the landscape of warfare as nations increasingly recognise the strategic advantages of controlling this vast frontier. As technology advances, space will no longer be viewed as a distant arena but as an integral part of military strategy. The deployment of space-based defense systems will play a crucial role in safeguarding national interests. These systems, equipped with advanced sensors and weaponry, will enhance capabilities for detection, tracking, and neutralising threats from both terrestrial and extraterrestrial sources. The integration of satellite systems for communication, reconnaissance, and navigation will further enable real-time decision-making, ensuring that military operations are not only efficient but also proactive.

Autonomous technologies, particularly drones and robotics, will redefine how military operations are conducted in space. The use of autonomous drones will facilitate surveillance and reconnaissance missions without risking human lives. These drones will be equipped with AI-driven intelligence analysis tools, allowing them to process vast amounts of data to identify and respond to threats swiftly. Additionally, advanced robotics will be employed for maintenance and repair of satellites and other space systems, ensuring that operational continuity is maintained even in hostile environments. This autonomy will significantly reduce the logistical burden on military personnel and enhance operational effectiveness.

Cyber warfare and cybersecurity will become paramount in the future of military operations in space. As military assets become increasingly reliant on interconnected systems, the risk of cyber-attacks will escalate. Protecting sensitive information and critical infrastructure in space will require robust cybersecurity measures. Military organisations will need to implement advanced biometric security and identification systems to ensure that only authorised personnel have access to critical systems. Furthermore, strategies for countering cyber threats will evolve, incorporating AI and quantum computing to identify vulnerabilities and predict potential attacks, creating a more resilient defense posture.

Augmented reality (AR) will revolutionise tactical training for military personnel, providing immersive simulations that mirror potential space conflict scenarios. This technology will allow soldiers to train in environments that replicate the complexities of space warfare, enhancing their readiness for real-world operations. AR can also be used to overlay critical information during missions, improving situational awareness and decision-making capabilities. As wearable technology becomes more prevalent, soldiers will have access to real-time data that can inform their actions on the battlefield, whether in space or on Earth.

Sustainable energy solutions will also play a vital role in future military operations in space, addressing the growing concern over the environmental impact of military activities. The development of efficient energy systems, such as solar power satellites, will ensure that military operations can be sustained over extended periods without reliance on traditional fuel sources. This shift not only enhances operational capabilities but also aligns military objectives with global sustainability goals. As nations invest in these technologies, the future of military operations in space will likely see a shift towards more responsible and sustainable practices, ensuring that the quest for superiority does not come at the expense of planetary health.

Chapter 22: Biometric security and identification

Biometric technologies refer to the measurement and statistical analysis of people's unique physical and behavioral characteristics. As warfare evolves, these technologies are increasingly integrated into military operations, enhancing security and operational efficiency. By leveraging unique biological traits such as fingerprints, facial recognition, iris scans, and voice patterns, militaries can streamline identification processes, ensuring that only authorised personnel access sensitive areas or information. This capability is crucial in modern combat environments where the speed and accuracy of identification can significantly impact mission success.

The rise of autonomous drone warfare has placed a premium on effective biometric systems. Drones equipped with biometric scanners can identify individuals in real-time, providing critical intelligence that can influence tactical decisions. For instance, during reconnaissance missions, drones can verify the identities of potential threats, enabling military forces to make informed choices about engagement. This technology reduces the risk of friendly fire incidents and enhances the overall effectiveness of drone operations, making biometrics an essential component of future military strategies.

Cyber warfare and cybersecurity efforts are also benefiting from advancements in biometric technologies. As cyber threats continue to evolve, the need for robust identification systems becomes paramount. Traditional password systems are increasingly vulnerable to hacking, but biometric authentication offers a higher level of security. By implementing biometric systems for access control in military networks, forces can better protect sensitive data and infrastructure. This shift not only fortifies defenses against cyber-attacks but also supports the integrity of information, ensuring that command and control systems remain secure.

Additionally, the integration of biometric technologies with advanced robotics in combat enhances situational awareness on the battlefield. Robots equipped with biometric sensors can assist soldiers by identifying allies and enemies, significantly reducing the risk of misidentification. This capability is particularly valuable in chaotic combat scenarios where visual identification may be difficult.

As the military explores these innovations, it must also address the ethical implications of biometric surveillance. The potential for misuse of biometric data raises concerns about privacy and civil liberties, particularly in conflict zones. Striking a balance between operational effectiveness and ethical considerations is essential. Future military strategies must incorporate robust policies that govern the use of biometric technologies to ensure they serve as tools for security and efficiency without infringing on individual rights. Thus, understanding biometric technologies is crucial for grasping their role in shaping the future of warfare.

Applications in military operations

MILITARY OPERATIONS today are increasingly integrating advanced technologies, fundamentally transforming how conflicts are managed and engaged. Skiving data crafts, for instance, are emerging as critical assets in this new landscape. These platforms harness data analytics to optimise reconnaissance and intelligence-gathering efforts, enabling commanders to make informed decisions rapidly. By utilising real-time data streams and sophisticated algorithms, militaries can achieve greater situational awareness, predict enemy movements, and enhance strategic planning. This approach not only minimises risks to personnel but also maximises operational efficiency in complex environments.

Autonomous drone warfare is revolutionizing the battlefield by providing unprecedented levels of precision and lethality. These drones can operate independently or in swarms, executing missions ranging from surveillance to targeted strikes with minimal human intervention. The integration of artificial intelligence into drone systems allows for advanced target recognition and engagement capabilities, reducing collateral damage and increasing mission success rates. As autonomous drones become more sophisticated, they will continue to play a pivotal role in military operations, enabling forces to project power with enhanced speed and effectiveness.

Cyber warfare and cybersecurity are critical components of modern military strategy. As conflicts move increasingly into the digital realm, the ability to protect and disrupt information systems becomes paramount. Military operations must prioritise the development of robust cybersecurity measures to safeguard sensitive data and maintain operational integrity. Simultaneously, offensive cyber capabilities are being refined to target adversary communications and infrastructure. This dual approach enhances tactical effectiveness while also protecting against potential cyber threats, making it a cornerstone of contemporary military engagements.

Advanced robotics are set to redefine combat dynamics, providing support across various operational theaters. From bomb disposal units to logistical support, robotic systems reduce the risk to human soldiers while performing high-risk tasks. These robots are often equipped with AI-driven decision-making capabilities, enabling them to operate autonomously in unpredictable environments. As robotics technology evolves, we can expect to see an increasing reliance on these systems in direct combat roles, further altering the traditional battlefield landscape.

Lastly, the incorporation of augmented reality (AR) into tactical training represents a significant advancement in preparing military personnel for future conflicts. AR systems can simulate real-world scenarios, allowing soldiers to practice and hone their skills in a controlled yet realistic environment. This technology enhances individual soldier capabilities and also improves team coordination and strategy execution.

Privacy and ethical concerns

PRIVACY AND ETHICAL concerns in the context of future warfare technologies are increasingly becoming focal points of discussion as military strategies evolve alongside advancements in data crafts, autonomous systems, and cyber warfare. The integration of sophisticated technologies such as AI-driven intelligence analysis and wearable technology for soldiers raises significant implications for individual privacy and the ethical frameworks governing military operations. As the boundaries between civilian and military applications blur, it is essential to consider how these innovations may infringe upon personal rights and freedoms while enhancing combat effectiveness.

The deployment of autonomous drones in warfare introduces complex ethical dilemmas surrounding accountability and the potential for unintended consequences. With the ability to conduct surveillance and engage targets without direct human intervention, questions arise about who is responsible for the actions of these machines. As military operations become more reliant on data-driven decision-making, the risk of algorithmic biases influencing outcomes increases, potentially leading to wrongful targeting or collateral damage. This necessitates a robust ethical framework to guide the development and deployment of such technologies, ensuring that they adhere to international humanitarian laws and respect for human dignity.

Cyber warfare presents another layer of privacy and ethical concerns, particularly regarding the collection and analysis of vast amounts of data. Governments and military organisations often justify surveillance activities under the guise of national security, yet this can lead to the erosion of civil liberties. As cyber capabilities become more sophisticated, the potential for invasive monitoring of both enemy and civilian populations grows. This raises critical questions about the balance between security and privacy, the accountability of those who wield these tools, and the need for transparency in operations that can affect millions of lives.

The advent of biometric security and identification technologies further complicates the ethical landscape. While these systems can enhance operational security and access control, they also pose significant risks to individual privacy. The collection and storage of biometric data, such as fingerprints and facial recognition, can lead to misuse or unauthorised access, creating vulnerabilities for both soldiers and civilians. As militaries adopt these technologies, it is vital to implement strong data protection measures and ethical guidelines to prevent abuse and ensure that privacy rights are upheld.

In conclusion, as military operations increasingly rely on advanced technologies, the necessity for a comprehensive approach to privacy and ethical concerns becomes paramount. Stakeholders must engage in ongoing dialogue to develop policies and frameworks that address these issues, promoting responsible innovation while safeguarding individual rights. By prioritising ethical considerations alongside technological advancements, the military of the future can pursue operational effectiveness without compromising the principles of privacy and human rights that underpin democratic societies.

Chapter 23: Sustainable energy solutions for military operations

The importance of sustainability in the military has become increasingly evident as global challenges such as climate change and resource scarcity shape the operational landscape. As military forces around the world adapt to these challenges, the need for sustainable practices is paramount. Sustainability not only enhances operational efficiency but also ensures the longevity of resources and minimizes the environmental impact of military activities. By integrating sustainability into military strategies, the armed forces can maintain readiness while addressing the pressing issues of environmental responsibility.

Sustainable energy solutions are a key component of modern military operations. The military's traditional reliance on fossil fuels poses both logistical challenges and environmental risks. As the demand for energy continues to rise, military leaders are exploring alternative energy sources such as solar, wind, and biofuels. These renewable energy options not only reduce the carbon footprint of military operations but also improve energy security by decreasing dependence on vulnerable supply chains. Implementing sustainable energy practices allows military forces to operate more independently and effectively in diverse environments.

In the realm of advanced robotics and autonomous systems, sustainability can also be a focal point. The development of energy-efficient drones and robots can significantly reduce the environmental impact of military operations. Innovations in battery technology and energy harvesting can extend the operational range of these systems while minimising their carbon footprint. Moreover, sustainable manufacturing practices in the production of military hardware can further enhance the overall sustainability of military capabilities, ensuring that technological advancements do not come at the expense of environmental health.

Cyber warfare and cybersecurity also intersect with sustainability in meaningful ways. The military's reliance on digital infrastructure necessitates robust cybersecurity measures to protect sensitive information and operational capabilities.

Innovative energy technologies are poised to revolutionise military operations in the future, offering enhanced efficiency, sustainability, and operational capabilities. As the military faces increasing scrutiny over its environmental impact, the development and deployment of alternative energy sources are becoming imperative. Renewable energy solutions, such as solar, wind, and advanced battery systems, are being integrated into military infrastructures, reducing reliance on traditional fossil fuels. These innovations not only lower operational costs but also enhance energy security, ensuring that troops can operate effectively even in remote or contested environments.

One of the most promising avenues in innovative energy technologies is the application of advanced battery systems, including solid-state and lithium-sulfur batteries. These batteries offer higher energy densities and faster charging times, which are critical for powering a new generation of autonomous drones and robotic systems. As military operations increasingly rely on these technologies for intelligence, surveillance, and reconnaissance missions, the need for reliable and high-capacity energy sources becomes paramount. Enhanced battery performance can extend the operational range and endurance of unmanned aerial vehicles, enabling them to conduct prolonged missions without the need for frequent recharging or logistical support.

In addition to battery advancements, the integration of energy harvesting technologies is gaining traction within military contexts. This includes systems that convert ambient energy, such as kinetic energy from soldier movements or thermal energy from equipment, into usable power. By incorporating energy harvesting technologies, soldiers can reduce their dependence on resupply missions for batteries and other energy sources, allowing for greater mobility and flexibility on the battlefield. This approach aligns with the military's broader goals of enhancing operational efficiency while minimising logistical burdens.

The emergence of microgrids is another innovative solution that facilitates decentralized energy management for military installations. Microgrids, powered by a combination of renewable sources and efficient storage systems, enable bases to operate independently from traditional energy grids. This is especially critical in conflict zones where infrastructure may be compromised. By leveraging microgrids, military installations can enhance their resilience and operational capability, ensuring that essential systems remain functional even during power disruptions or cyberattacks on energy infrastructure.

Finally, the integration of sustainable energy solutions extends beyond immediate operational benefits; it also addresses broader strategic concerns. As militaries around the world confront the realities of climate change and its implications for global security, adopting innovative energy technologies can enhance readiness and adaptability. The transition toward greener energy solutions bolsters military effectiveness and also positions armed forces as leaders in sustainability efforts, contributing to international stability and peace. Ultimately, these advancements in energy technology represent a critical component in the ongoing evolution of military operations in an increasingly complex global landscape.

Case Studies on Sustainable Practices

CASE STUDIES ON SUSTAINABLE practices in military operations illustrate the evolving landscape of defense strategies that prioritize environmental stewardship alongside operational effectiveness. One notable example is the U.S. Army's implementation of solar energy solutions in combat zones. By deploying solar panels in forward operating bases, the Army has significantly reduced its dependence on fuel convoys, which are often vulnerable to enemy attacks. This shift not only enhances energy security but also minimizes the carbon footprint of military operations, demonstrating a practical application of sustainable energy solutions in warfare.

Another compelling case study involves the use of advanced robotics for logistics and supply chain management within military frameworks. The U.S. Navy has experimented with autonomous robotic systems designed to transport supplies on ships and in port environments. These systems reduce the need for human intervention in potentially hazardous areas, thereby enhancing safety and efficiency. Furthermore, the implementation of these robots has led to a decrease in resource consumption, as they are engineered to operate with precision and minimal waste, aligning military operations with broader environmental sustainability goals.

Cybersecurity practices also serve as a case study in sustainable military operations. The U.S. Department of Defense has increasingly focused on developing resilient cyber infrastructure to protect sensitive information against evolving threats. By investing in renewable energy sources to power data centers and employing advanced AI-driven intelligence analysis, the military enhances its operational capabilities and also contributes to a more sustainable technological ecosystem. This approach ensures that military installations can maintain operations during disruptions, showcasing a commitment to sustainability in the realm of cybersecurity.

The integration of wearable technology for soldiers provides another insight into sustainable practices within the military. Case studies on the use of such technology highlight the potential for innovation to drive sustainability in military operations.

Finally, the exploration of space-based defense systems offers a forward-looking perspective on sustainable military practices. The increasing reliance on satellite technology for communications, reconnaissance, and navigation underscores the need for sustainable energy solutions in space. Projects aimed at developing solar-powered satellites exemplify how the military can harness renewable resources to ensure operational continuity while minimising environmental impact.

Chapter 24: The future of warfare

The landscape of military technology is undergoing a profound transformation, driven largely by advancements in data analysis and automation. Predicting trends in this sphere requires an understanding of how emerging technologies will shape future warfare. Skiving data crafts, which utilise vast amounts of data to inform tactical decisions, are at the forefront of this evolution. These systems enhance situational awareness and allow military planners to anticipate enemy movements, optimising resource allocation and operational effectiveness. The integration of big data analytics into military operations will not only improve decision-making but also enable predictive modeling that can foresee future conflicts and their potential outcomes.

Future military operations will likely see a rise in swarm technology, where multiple drones work in unison to carry out complex missions. This trend towards autonomy raises important ethical and strategic questions regarding accountability and the potential for unintended consequences in combat scenarios. As these technologies evolve, military organisations will need to develop robust frameworks to govern their use, ensuring that they are employed responsibly.

Cyber warfare and cybersecurity are equally crucial in the future of military operations. The rise of interconnected systems has created new vulnerabilities, making it essential for military forces to invest in advanced cybersecurity measures. As adversaries increasingly target critical infrastructure and military networks, the ability to predict and mitigate cyber threats will become paramount. Furthermore, AI-driven intelligence analysis will play a pivotal role in identifying emerging cyber threats and formulating countermeasures. The integration of machine learning into cybersecurity protocols will allow for faster detection of anomalies and more effective responses to potential attacks.

Advanced robotics in combat will also redefine how military engagements are conducted. Robots are expected to take on more complex roles, from logistics support to direct engagement in combat scenarios. Their utilisation will not only reduce the risk to human soldiers but also enhance operational capabilities in challenging environments. The ongoing development of wearable technology for soldiers, including smart uniforms equipped with biometric sensors and communication tools, will further augment situational awareness and physical readiness on the battlefield. As these technologies mature, they will empower soldiers with real-time data, improving their performance and safety.

Lastly, the advent of quantum computing holds immense promise for military strategy. Its unparalleled processing power could revolutionise data encryption, secure communications, and complex simulations for strategic planning. Space-based defense systems are also on the horizon, offering new avenues for surveillance and missile defense. As militaries strive for sustainable energy solutions, innovations in renewable energy sources will become vital for long-term operations, reducing dependency on traditional fuel supplies. Collectively, these trends highlight an era of rapid technological advancement that will fundamentally alter the nature of military operations, requiring continuous adaptation and foresight from military leaders and policymakers.

The role of global collaboration

GLOBAL COLLABORATION has become an indispensable element in shaping the future landscape of warfare, particularly as nations increasingly engage in complex conflicts that transcend borders and traditional military paradigms. The rapid advancement of technology, including autonomous systems, AI-driven analytics, and quantum computing, necessitates a unified approach to enhance operational effectiveness and ensure security. In this context, military forces around the world must forge partnerships that enable shared access to critical data, resources, and expertise, ultimately fostering a synchronised response to emerging threats.

One of the most significant aspects of global collaboration is the sharing of intelligence and data across nations. In the realm of cyber warfare and cybersecurity, for instance, the interconnected nature of digital infrastructure means that a threat in one nation can have far-reaching implications for others. Collaborative intelligence-sharing initiatives can help identify vulnerabilities, anticipate attacks, and implement preemptive measures. Countries can leverage advanced AI-driven intelligence analysis tools to process vast amounts of data collaboratively, enhancing their ability to respond to cyber threats and safeguard national interests.

Advancements in autonomous drone warfare and advanced robotics in combat are revolutionising military operations. Collaborative efforts in developing and testing these technologies can lead to improved operational capabilities and reduced risks for personnel. Joint exercises and training programs involving multiple nations can also facilitate the exchange of best practices, ensuring that armed forces are well-prepared to operate in complex environments. By pooling resources and expertise, countries can accelerate innovation and advance the development of cutting-edge technologies that redefine the battlefield.

The integration of augmented reality for tactical training presents another area where global collaboration can yield substantial benefits. By sharing training methodologies and technological advancements, military forces can enhance the effectiveness of their training programs, preparing soldiers for the realities of modern combat. Collaborative platforms can allow for the creation of shared virtual environments where troops from different nations can engage in simulated combat scenarios, fostering interoperability and mutual understanding. This approach not only strengthens the skills of individual soldiers but also enhances the cohesion of multinational forces in joint operations.

Finally, sustainable energy solutions for military operations are becoming increasingly critical as nations seek to minimize their environmental impact while maintaining operational readiness. Collaborative research and development in renewable energy technologies can lead to innovative solutions that power military assets more efficiently. By sharing knowledge and resources, countries can develop sustainable energy systems that support not only military objectives but also contribute to broader global efforts toward environmental sustainability. In an age where the consequences of warfare extend beyond the battlefield, global collaboration stands as a crucial pillar in the quest for effective and responsible military operations in the future.

Preparing for the unknown in warfare

IN THE RAPIDLY EVOLVING landscape of modern warfare, the concept of preparing for the unknown has become increasingly critical. As military operations integrate advanced technologies such as skiving data crafts, autonomous drones, and AI-driven intelligence analysis, the unpredictability of warfare escalates. This necessitates a paradigm shift in how military forces train, plan, and execute missions. Embracing a mindset that prioritises flexibility, adaptability, and continuous learning is essential for overcoming the challenges posed by these transformative technologies.

The integration of augmented reality for tactical training exemplifies how military forces can prepare for uncertain scenarios. By utilising immersive training environments that simulate real-world conditions, soldiers can engage in realistic combat exercises without the inherent risks of live operations. This technology not only enhances individual soldier skills but also fosters teamwork and decision-making under pressure. As scenarios evolve with the introduction of advanced robotics and cyber warfare tactics, augmented reality can be adapted to reflect these changes, ensuring that troops remain prepared for the unexpected.

Another vital aspect of preparing for the unknown is the implementation of biometric security and identification systems. As forces increasingly rely on advanced technologies for operations, ensuring the integrity of personnel and equipment becomes paramount. Biometric systems provide a reliable method for authenticating individuals and securing access to sensitive information. This technology can help mitigate the risks associated with espionage, infiltration, and insider threats, which are often difficult to predict. By investing in robust cybersecurity measures alongside biometric solutions, military organizations can create a more secure operational environment.

The advent of quantum computing in military strategy introduces another layer of complexity and potential uncertainty. Quantum computing's ability to process vast amounts of data at unprecedented speeds can revolutionise intelligence analysis, yet it also poses unique challenges. Adversaries may leverage similar technologies, leading to an arms race in quantum capabilities. Therefore, military forces must not only invest in quantum computing research but also develop strategies to counteract potential threats arising from its misuse. This proactive approach will help ensure that military operations are prepared for any unforeseen developments in this realm.

Finally, sustainable energy solutions for military operations are essential for preparing for the unknown in an era where resource scarcity and environmental considerations are increasingly relevant. As conflicts may arise in regions affected by climate change, military forces must develop strategies that ensure operational sustainability. Investing in renewable energy sources and efficient energy management systems can enhance resilience in the face of logistical challenges. By prioritising sustainability, military operations can maintain effectiveness while minimising their environmental impact, thus preparing for a future where resource availability may be unpredictable.

Also by DM Ole Kiminta

How the Western Democracies failed the world
How the Western Democracies failed the world
Shadows in the water: Supporting refugees in their homelands
Availing Concerted global responsibility for Afghan women's rights
Tethered to the kitchen: Concerted global responsibility for Afghanistan
women's rights
Dissuading Global War Mongers:
Dissuading war mongers

About the Author

DM Ole Kiminta is a Canadian of Maasai heritage. He spent many years working in USA, Britain and in Canada. He is an Industrial engineer, Petroleum engineer and Chemical engineer. Ole Kiminta was educated in USA and United Kingdom. Some of his published research work include Material science, carbon fibres and other composite materials, Polymeric materials, and Particle technology. He currently works for the Canadian government and lives in Toronto Canada with his family.

www.ingramcontent.com/pod-product-compliance
Lightning Source LLC
Chambersburg PA
CBHW071319130726

47996CB00002B/540